AS ONE IS

To Free the Mind
from All Conditioning

J. Krishnamurti

Ojai Public Talks, 1955

HOHM PRESS
Chino Valley, Arizona

Cover design: Kim Johansen
Layout and design: Zachary Parker, Kadak Graphics

Library of Congress Cataloging-in-Publication Data

Krishnamurti, J. (Jiddu), 1895-1986.
  As one is : to free the mind from all conditioning / J. Krishnamur.
    p. cm.
  "Ojai public talks, 1955".
  ISBN 1-890772-62-3 (trade pbk. : alk. paper)
  1. Krishnamurti, J. (Jiddu), 1895-1986. I. Title.
  B5134.K754A5 2007
  181'.4--dc22

                      2006036360

HOHM PRESS
P.O. Box 4410
Chino Valley, AZ 86323
800-381-2700
http://www.hohmpress.com

This book was printed in the U.S.A. on recycled, acid-free paper using soy ink.

1 2 3 4 5

Contents

To stand alone is to be uncorrupted, innocent, free of all tradition, of dogma, of opinion, of what another says, and so on. Such a mind does not seek because there is nothing to seek; being free, such a mind is completely still without a want, without movement. But this state is not to be achieved; it isn't a thing that you buy through discipline; it doesn't come into being by giving up sex, or practicing a certain yoga. It comes into being only when there is understanding of the ways of the self, the 'me', which shows itself through the conscious mind in every day activity, and also in the unconscious. What matters is to understand for oneself, not through the direction of others, the total content of consciousness, which is conditioned, which is the result of society, of religion, of various impacts, impressions, memories—to understand all that conditioning and be free of it. But there is no "how" to be free. If you ask how to be free, you are not listening.[1]

These words challenge the movement of human consciousness conditioned traditionally to accept the idea of spiritual progress, of achievement through time, and methods to reach there. It challenges the deep conditioning of *how* for the inner life, and its corollaries: spiritual authority, belief, conformity, the idea of *seeking* itself.

1 page 27

J. Krishnamurti

These talks point to understanding how one is, just as one is, in the living moments of daily life—not how one should be, as defined by cultural values, religious ideals and self-projected futures. Such discoveries ask ourselves to be understood, not this text to be accepted as true. In the last of these talks a questioner who has reached an impasse asks "What now?" Embarking on such an uncharted sea, there is this reply to contemplate:

Are you experimenting with my teachings, or are you experimenting with yourself? I hope you see the difference. If you are experimenting with what I am saying, then you must come to, "What now?" because then you are trying to achieve a result which you think I have. You think I have something which you do not have, and that if you experiment with what I am saying, you also will get it—which is what most of us do. We approach these things with a commercial mentality—I will do this in order to get that. I will worship, meditate, sacrifice in order to get something.

Now, you are not practicing my teachings. I have nothing to say. Or rather, all that I am saying is: Observe your own mind, see to what depths the mind can go; therefore you are important, not the teachings. It is important for you to find out your own ways of thinking and what that thinking implies, as I have been trying to point out this morning. And if you are really observing your own thinking, if you are watching, experimenting, discovering, letting go, dying each day to everything that you have gathered, then you will never put that question, "What now?"[2]

2 page 136

Foreword

These eight talks were spoken without notes, *ex tempore*, in the shade of a grove of oak trees in the summer of 1955 before an audience of perhaps several hundred in the Ojai valley in California. Krishnamurti first visited the valley in 1922 and lived there, when not traveling elsewhere to speak, until his death in 1986. He died at the age of 91 in Pine Cottage, which today is next door to the Krishnamurti Archives in Ojai at the foot of the Topa Topa mountain bluffs. He founded several foundations around the world to preserve and keep available his talks, writings and dialogues. As of the date of this edition, more information as well as audio, video and text is available at jkrishnamurti.org.

"When the mind is free from all conditioning, then you will find that there comes the creativity of reality, of God, or what you will, and it is only such a mind, a mind which is constantly experiencing this creativity, that can bring about a different outlook, different values, a different world."

Throughout the world we have many grave problems, and even though welfare states may be created, and the politicians may bring about a superficial peace of coexistence—with economic prosperity in a country of this kind where there is booming production and the promise of a happy future—I do not think that our problems can so easily be solved. We want these problems to be solved, and we look to others to solve them—to religious teachers,. to analysts, to leaders—or else we rely on tradition, or we turn to various books, philosophies. And I presume that is why you are here—to be told what to do. Or you hope that through listening to explanations, you will comprehend the problems that each one of us is confronted with. But I think you will be making a grave mistake if you expect that by casually listening to one or two talks, without paying much attention, you will be guided to the comprehension of our many problems. It is not at all my intention merely to explain verbally or intellectually the problems that we are confronted with; on the contrary, what we shall attempt to do during these talks is to go much deeper into the fundamental issue which makes all these problems so complicated, so infinitely painful and sorrowful.

Please have the patience to listen without being carried away by words, or objecting to one or two phrases or ideas. One must have immense patience to find out what is true. Most of us are impatient to get on, to find a result, to achieve a success, a goal, a certain state of happiness, or to experience something to which the mind can cling. But what is needed, I think, is a patience and a perseverance to seek without an end. Most of us are seeking; that is why we are here, but in our search we want to find something, a result, a goal, a state of being in which we can be happy, peaceful; so our search is already determined, is it not? When we seek, we are seeking something which we want, so our search is already established, predetermined, and therefore it is no longer a search. I think it is very important to understand this. When the mind seeks a particular state, a solution to a problem, when it seeks God, truth, or desires a certain experience, whether mystical or any other kind, it has already conceived what it wants; and because it has already conceived, formulated, what it is seeking, its search is infinitely futile. And it is one of the most difficult things to free the mind from this desire to find a result.

It seems to me that our many problems cannot be solved except through a fundamental revolution of the mind, for such a revolution alone can bring about the realization of that which is truth. Therefore, it is important to understand the operation of one's own mind, not self-analytically or introspectively, but by being aware of its total process; and that is what I would like to discuss during these talks. If we do not see ourselves as we are, if we do not understand the thinker—the entity that seeks, that is perpetually asking, demanding, questioning, trying to find out, the entity that is creating the problem, the 'I', the self, the ego—then our thought, our search, will have no meaning. As long as one's instrument of thinking is not clear, is perverted, conditioned, whatever one thinks is bound to be limited, narrow.

So our problem is how to free the mind from all conditioning, not how to condition it better. Do you understand? Most of us are seeking a better conditioning. The communists, the Catholics, the Protestants, and the various other sects throughout the world, including the Hindus and Buddhists, are all seeking to condition the mind according to a nobler, a more virtuous, unselfish, or religious pattern. Everyone throughout the world, surely, is trying to condition the mind in a better way, and there is never a question of freeing the mind from all conditioning. But it seems to me that until the mind is free from all conditioning, that is, as long as it is conditioned as a Christian, a Buddhist, a Hindu, a communist, or whatnot, there must be problems.

Surely, it is possible to find out what is real, or if there is such a thing as God, only when the mind is free from all conditioning. The mere occupation of a conditioned mind with God, with truth, with love, has really no meaning at all, for such a mind can function only within the field of its conditioning. The communist who does not believe in God thinks in one way, and the man who believes in God, who is occupied with a dogma, thinks in another way; but the minds of both are conditioned; therefore, neither can think freely, and all their protestations, their theories and beliefs have very little meaning. So religion is not a matter of going to church, of having certain beliefs and dogmas. Religion may be something entirely different; it may be the total freeing of the mind from all this vast tradition of centuries, for it is only a free mind that can find truth, reality, that which is beyond the projections of the mind.

This is not a particular theory of mine, as we can see from what is happening in the world. The communists want to settle the problems of life in one way, the Hindus in another, and the Christians in still another; so their minds are conditioned. Your mind is conditioned as a Christian, whether you will acknowledge it or not. You may superficially break away from the tradition of Christianity, but the deep layers of the unconscious are full of that tradition; they are conditioned by centuries of education according to a particular pattern; and surely, a mind that would find something beyond, if there is such a thing, must first be free of all conditioning.

So during these talks we are not discussing self-improvement in any way, nor are we concerned with the improvement of the pattern; we are not seeking to condition the mind in a nobler pattern, nor in a pattern of wider social significance. On the contrary, we are trying to find out how to free the mind, the total consciousness, from all conditioning, for unless that happens, there can be no experiencing of reality. You may talk about reality, you may read innumerable volumes about it, read all the sacred books of the East and of the West, but until the mind is aware of its own process, until it sees itself functioning in a particular pattern and is able to be free from that conditioning, obviously all search is in vain.

So it seems to me of the greatest importance to begin with ourselves, to be aware of our own conditioning. And how extraordinarily difficult it is to know that one is conditioned! Superficially, on the upper levels of the mind, we may be aware that we are conditioned; we may break away from one pattern and take on another, give up Christianity and become a communist, leave Catholicism and join some other equally tyrannical group, thinking that we are evolving, growing towards reality. On the contrary, it is merely an exchange of prisons.

And yet that is what most of us want—to find a secure place in our ways of thinking. We want to pursue a set pattern and be undisturbed in our thoughts, in our actions. But it is only the mind that is capable of patiently observing its own conditioning and being free from its conditioning—it is only such a mind that is able to have a revolution, a radical transformation, and thereby to discover that which is infinitely beyond the mind, beyond all our desires, our vanities and pursuits. Without self-knowledge, without knowing oneself as one is—not as one would like to be, which is merely an illusion, an idealistic escape—without knowing the ways of one's thinking, all one's motives, one's thoughts, one's innumerable responses, it is not possible to understand and go beyond this whole process of thinking.

You have taken a lot of trouble to come here on a hot evening to listen to the talk. And I wonder if you do listen at all. What is listening? I think it is important to go into it a little, if you do not mind. Do you really listen, or are you interpreting what is being said in terms of your own understanding? Are you capable of listening to anybody? Or is it that in the process of listening, various thoughts, opinions, arise so that your own knowledge and experience intervene between what is being said and your comprehension of it?

I think it is important to understand the difference between attention and concentration. Concentration implies choice, does it not? You are trying to concentrate on what I am saying, so your mind is focused, made narrow, and other thoughts intervene; so there is not an actual listening but a battle going on in the mind, a conflict between what you are hearing and your desire to translate it, to apply what I am talking about, and so on. Whereas, attention is something entirely different. In attention there is no focusing, no choice; there is complete awareness without any interpretation. And if we can listen so attentively, completely, to what is being said, then that very attention brings about the miracle of change within the mind itself.

What we are talking about is something of immense importance because unless there is a fundamental revolution in each one of us, I do not see how we can bring about a vast, radical change in the world. And surely, that radical change is essential. Mere economic revolution, whether communistic or socialistic, is of no importance at all. There can be only a religious revolution, and the religious revolution cannot take place if the mind is merely conforming to the pattern of a previous conditioning. As long as one is a Christian or a Hindu, there can be no fundamental revolution in this true religious sense of the word. And we do need such a revolution. When the mind is free from all conditioning, then you will find that there comes the creativity of reality, of God, or what you will, and it is only such a mind, a mind which is constantly experiencing this creativity, that can bring about a different outlook, different values, a different world.

And so it is important to understand oneself, is it not? Self-knowledge is the beginning of wisdom. Self-

First Talk

knowledge is not according to some psychologist, book, or philosopher but it is to know oneself as one is from moment to moment. Do you understand? To know oneself is to observe what one thinks, how one feels, not just superficially, but to be deeply aware of what is without condemnation, without judgment, without evaluation or comparison. Try it and you will see how extraordinarily difficult it is for a mind that has been trained for centuries to compare, to condemn, to judge, to evaluate, to stop that whole process and simply to observe *what is*; but unless this takes place, not only at the superficial level, but right through the whole content of consciousness, there can be no delving into the profundity of the mind.

Please, if you are really here to understand what is being said, it is this that we are concerned with and nothing else. Our problem is not what societies you should belong to, what kind of activities you should indulge in, what books you should read, and all that superficial business, but how to free the mind from conditioning. The mind is not merely the waking consciousness that is occupied with daily activities, but also the deep layers of the unconscious in which there is the whole residue of the past, of tradition, of racial instincts. All that is the mind, and unless that total consciousness is free right through, our search, our inquiry, our discovery, will be limited, narrow, petty.

So the mind is conditioned right through; there is no part of the mind which is not conditioned, and our problem is: Can such a mind free itself? And who is the entity that can free it? Do you understand the problem? The mind is the total consciousness with all its different layers of knowledge, of acquisition, of tradition, of

9

racial instincts, of memory; and can such a mind free itself? Or can the mind be free only when it sees that it is conditioned and that any movement from this conditioning is still another form of conditioning? I hope you are following all this. If not, we shall discuss it in the days to come.

The mind is completely conditioned—which is an obvious fact if you come to think about it. It is not my invention, it is a fact. We belong to a particular society; we were brought up according to a particular ideology with certain dogmas, traditions; and the vast influence of culture, of society, is continually conditioning the mind. How can such a mind be free, since any movement of the mind to be free is the result of its conditioning and must therefore bring about further conditioning? There is only one answer. The mind can be free only when it is completely still. Though it has problems, innumerable urges, conflicts, ambitions, if—through self-knowledge, through watching itself without acceptance or condemnation—the mind is choicelessly aware of its own process, then out of that awareness there comes an astonishing silence, a quietness of the mind in which there is no movement of any kind. It is only then that the mind is free because it is no longer desiring anything; it is no longer seeking; it is no longer pursuing a goal, an ideal—which are all the projections of a conditioned mind. And if you ever come to that understanding, in which there can be no self-deception, then you will find that there is a possibility of the coming into being of that extraordinary thing called creativity. Then only can the mind realize that which is measureless, which may be called God, truth, or what you will—the word has very little meaning. You may be socially prosperous, you may have innumerable possessions, cars, houses, refrigerators, superficial peace, but unless that which is measureless comes into being, there will always be sorrow. Freeing the mind from conditioning is the ending of sorrow.

There are many questions here, and what is the function of asking a question and receiving an answer? Do we solve any problem by asking a question? What is a problem? Please follow this, think with me. What is a problem? A problem comes into being only when the mind is occupied with something, does it not? If I have a problem, what does it mean? Let's say that my mind is occupied from morning till night with envy, with jealousy, with sex, or what you will. It is the occupation of the mind with an object that creates the problem. The envy may be a fact, but it is the occupation of the mind with the fact that creates the problem, the conflict. Isn't that so?

Let's say I am envious, or I have a violent urge of some kind or another. The envy expresses itself; there is conflict, and then my mind is occupied with the conflict—how to be free of it, how to resolve it, what to do about it. It is the occupation of the mind with envy that creates the problem, not envy itself—which we will go into presently, the whole significance of envy. Our problem, then, is not the fact but occupation with the fact. And can the mind be free from occupation? Is the mind capable of dealing with the fact without being occupied with it? We shall examine this question of occupation as we go along. It is really very interesting to watch one's mind in operation.

So, in considering these questions together, we are trying to liberate the mind from occupation, which means looking at the fact without being occupied with it. That is, if I have a particular compulsion, can I look at that compulsion without being occupied with it? Please, you watch your own peculiar compulsion of irritability or whatever it be. Can you look at it without the mind being occupied with it? Occupation implies the effort to resolve that compulsion, does it not? You are condemning it, comparing it with something else, trying to alter it, overcome it. In other words, trying to do something about your compulsion is occupation, is it not? But can you look at the fact that you have a particular compulsion, an urge, a desire, look at it without comparing, without judging, and hence not set going the whole process of occupation?

Psychologically, it is very interesting to observe this—how the mind is incapable of looking at a fact like envy without bringing in the vast complex of opinions, judgments, evaluations with which the mind is occupied—so we never resolve the fact but multiply the problems. I hope I am making myself clear. And I think it is important for us to understand this process of occupation because there is a much deeper factor behind it, which is the fear of not being occupied. Whether a mind is occupied with God, with truth, with sex, or with drink, its quality is essentially the same. The man who thinks about God and becomes a hermit may be socially more significant; he may have a greater value to society than the drunkard, but both are occupied, and a mind that is occupied is never free to discover what is truth. Please don't reject or accept what I am saying; look at it, find out. If each one of us can really attend to this one thing, give our full attention to the whole process of the mind's occupation with any problem without trying to free the mind from occupation, which is merely another way of being occupied—if we can understand this process completely, totally, then I think the problem itself will become irrelevant. When the mind is free from occupation with the problem, free to observe, to be aware of the whole issue, then the problem itself can be solved comparatively easily.

Questioner: All our troubles seem to arise from desire, but can we ever be free from desire? Is desire inherent in us, or is it a product of the mind?

Krishnamurti: What is desire? And why do we separate desire from the mind? And who is the entity that says, "Desire creates problems; therefore, I must be free from desire"? Do you follow? We have to understand what desire is, not ask how to get rid of desire because it creates trouble or whether it is a product of the mind. First we must know what desire is, and then we can go into it more deeply. What is desire? How does desire arise? I shall explain and you will see, but don't merely listen to my words. Actually experience the thing that we are talking about as we go along, and then it will have significance.

How does desire come into being? Surely, it comes into being through perception or seeing, contact, sensation, and then desire. Isn't that so? First you see a car, then there is contact, sensation, and finally the desire to own the car, to drive it. Please follow this slowly, patiently. Then, in trying to get that car, which is desire, there is conflict. So in the very fulfillment of desire there is conflict, there is pain, suffering, joy, and you want to hold the pleasure and discard the pain. This is what is actually taking place with each one of us. The entity created by desire, the entity who is identified with pleasure, says, "I must get rid of that which is not pleasurable, which is painful." We never say, "I want to get rid of pain and pleasure." We want to retain pleasure and discard pain, but desire creates both, does it not? Desire, which comes into being through perception, contact, and sensation, is identified as the 'me' who wants to hold on to the pleasurable and discard that which is painful. But the painful and the pleasurable are equally the outcome of desire, which is part of the mind—it is not outside of the mind—and as long as there is an entity which says, "I want to hold on to this and discard that," there must be conflict. Because we want to get rid of all the painful desires and hold on to those which are primarily pleasurable, worthwhile, we never consider the whole problem of desire. And when we say, "I must get rid of desire," who is the entity that is trying to get rid of something? Is not that entity also the outcome of desire? Do you understand all this?

Please, as I said at the beginning of the talk, you must have infinite patience to understand these things. To fundamental questions, there is no absolute answer of yes or no. What is important is to put a fundamental question, not to find an answer, and if we are capable of looking at that fundamental question without seeking an answer, then that very observation of the fundamental brings about understanding.

So our problem is not how to be free from the desires which are painful while holding on to those which are pleasurable but to understand the whole nature of desire.

This brings up the question: What is conflict? And who is the entity that is always choosing between the pleasurable and the painful? The entity whom we call the 'me', the self, the ego, the mind, which says, "This is pleasure, that is pain; I will hold on to the pleasurable and reject the painful"—is not that entity still desire? But if we are capable of looking at the whole field of desire, and not in terms of keeping or getting rid of something, then we shall find that desire has quite a different significance.

Desire creates contradiction, and the mind that is at all alert does not like to live in contradiction; therefore, it tries to get rid of desire. But if the mind can understand desire without trying to brush it away, without saying, "This is a better desire and that is a worse one, I am going to keep this and discard the other"; if it can be aware of the whole field of desire without rejecting, without choosing, without condemning, then you will see that the mind is desire; it is not separate from desire. If you really understand this, the mind becomes very quiet; desires come, but they no longer have impact; they are no longer of great significance; they do not take root in the mind and create problems. The mind reacts; otherwise, it is not alive, but the reaction is superficial and does not take root. That is why it is important to understand this whole process of desire in which most of us are caught. Being caught, we feel the contradiction, the infinite pain of it, so we struggle against desire, and the struggle creates duality. Whereas, if we can look at desire without judgment, without evaluation or condemnation, then we shall find that it no longer takes root. The mind that gives soil to problems can never find that which is real. So the issue is not how to resolve desire but

J. Krishnamurti

to understand it, and one can understand it only when there is no condemnation of it. Only the mind that is not occupied with desire can understand desire.

"Everywhere society is conditioning the individual, and this conditioning takes the form of self-improvement, which is really the perpetuation of the 'me', the ego, in different forms. Self-improvement may be gross, or it may be very, very refined when it becomes the practice of virtue, goodness, the so-called love of one's neighbor, but essentially it is the continuance of the 'me', which is a product of the conditioning influences of society. All your endeavor has gone into becoming something, either here, if you can make it, or if not, in another world; but it is the same urge, the same drive to maintain and continue the self."

Second Talk in the Oak Grove
August 7, 1955

Perhaps it might be worthwhile, first of all, to talk over together what we mean by listening. You are here, apparently, to listen to and to understand what is being said, and I think it is important to find out how we listen because understanding depends on the manner of listening. As we listen, do we discuss with ourselves what is being said, interpreting it according to our own particular opinions, knowledge, and idiosyncrasies, or do we just listen attentively without any sense of interpretation at all? And what does it mean to pay attention? It seems to me quite important to differentiate between attention and concentration. Can we listen with an attention in which there is no interpretation, no opposition or acceptance, so that we understand totally what is being said? It is fairly obvious, I think, that if one can listen with complete attention, then that very attention brings about an extraordinary effect.

Surely, there are two ways of listening. One can superficially follow the words, see their meaning, and merely pursue the outward significance of the description; or one can listen to the description, to the verbal statement, and pursue it inwardly—that is, be aware of what is being said as a thing that one is directly experiencing in oneself. If one can do the latter—that is, if through the description one is able to experience directly the thing that is being said—then I think it will have great significance. Perhaps you will experiment with that as you are listening.

Throughout the world there is immense poverty, as in Asia, and enormous wealth, as in this country; there is cruelty, suffering, injustice, a sense of living in which there is no love. Seeing all this, what is one to do? What is the true approach to these innumerable problems? Religions everywhere have emphasized self-improvement, the cultivation of virtue, the acceptance of authority, the following of certain dogmas, beliefs, the making of great effort to conform. Not only religiously, but also socially and politically, there is the constant urge of self-improvement: I must be more noble, more gentle, more considerate, less violent. Society, with the help of religion, has brought about a culture of self-improvement in the widest sense of that word. That is what each one of us is trying to do all the time—we are trying to improve ourselves, which implies effort, discipline, conformity, competition, acceptance of authority, a sense of security, the justification of ambition. And self-improvement does produce certain obvious results; it makes one more socially inclined; it has social significance and no more, for self-improvement does not reveal the ultimate reality. I think it is very important to understand this.

The religions that we have do not help us to understand that which is the real because they are essentially based, not on the abandonment of the self, but on the improvement, the refinement of the self, which is the continuity of the self in different forms. It is only the very few who break away from society, not the outward trappings of society, but from all the implications of a society which is based on acquisitiveness, on envy, on comparison, competition. This society conditions the mind to a particular pattern of thought, the pattern of self-improvement, self-adjustment, self-sacrifice, and only those who are capable of breaking away from all conditioning can discover that which is not measurable by the mind.

Now, what do we mean by effort? We are all making effort; our social pattern is based on the effort to acquire, to understand more, to have more knowledge, and from that background of knowledge, to act. There is always an effort of self-improvement, of self-adjustment, of correction, this drive to fulfill, with its frustrations, fears, and miseries. According to this pattern, which we all know and of which we are a part, it is perfectly justified to be ambitious, to compete, to be envious, to pursue a particular result; and our society, whether in America, in Europe, or in India, is essentially based on that.

So does society, does culture in this widest sense, help the individual to find truth? Or is society detrimental to man, preventing him from discovering that which is truth? Surely, society as we know it, this culture in which we live and function, helps man to conform to a particular pattern, to be respectable, and it is the product of many wills. We have created this society; it has not come into being by itself. And does this society help the individual to find that which is truth, God—what name you will, the words do not matter—or must the individual set aside totally the culture, the values of society, to find that which is truth? Which does not mean—please let us remember this very clearly—that he becomes antisocial, does what he likes. On the contrary.

The present social structure is based on envy, on acquisitiveness, in which is implied conformity, acceptance of authority, the perpetual fulfillment of ambition, which is essentially the self, the 'me' striving to become something. Out of this stuff society is made, and its culture—the pleasant and the unpleasant, the beautiful and the ugly, the whole field of social endeavor—conditions the mind. You are the result of society. If you were born and trained in Russia through their particular form of education, you would deny God, you would accept certain patterns, as here you accept certain other patterns. Here you believe in God; you would be horrified if you did not; you would not be respectable.

So everywhere society is conditioning the individual, and this conditioning takes the form of self-improvement, which is really the perpetuation of the 'me', the ego, in different forms. Self-improvement may be gross, or it may be very, very refined when it becomes the practice of virtue, goodness, the so-called love of one's neighbor, but essentially it is the continuance of the 'me', which is a product of the conditioning influences of society. All your endeavor has gone into becoming something, either here, if you can make it, or if not, in another world; but it is the same urge, the same drive to maintain and continue the self.

When one sees all this—and I am not necessarily going into every detail of it—one inevitably asks oneself: Does society or culture exist to help man to discover that which may be called truth or God? What matters, surely, is to discover, to actually experience, something far beyond the mind, not merely to have a belief, which has no significance at all. And do so-called religions, the following of various teachers, disciplines, belonging to sects, cults, which are all, if you observe, within the field of social respectability—do any of those things help you to find that which is timeless bliss, timeless reality? If you do not merely listen to what is being said, agreeing or disagreeing, but ask yourself whether society helps you, not in the superficial sense of feeding you, clothing you, and giving you shelter, but fundamentally—if you are actually putting that question directly to yourself, which means that you are applying what is being said to yourself so that it becomes a direct experience and not merely a repetition of what you have heard or learned, then you will see that effort can exist only in the field of self-improvement. And effort is basically part of society, which conditions the mind according to a pattern in which effort is considered essential.

It is like this. If I am a scientist, I must study, I must know mathematics, I must know all that has been said before, I must have an immense accumulation of knowledge. My memory must be heightened, strengthened, and widened. But such a memory, such knowledge, actually prevents further discovery. It is only when I can forget the total acquisition of knowledge, wipe away all the information that I have acquired, which can be used later—it is only then that I can find something new. I cannot find anything new with the burden of the past, with the burden of knowledge, which is again an obvious psychological fact. And I am saying this because we approach reality, that extraordinary state of creativity, with all the burden of society, with the conditioning of a given culture, and so we never discover anything new. Surely, that which is the sublime, the eternal, must always be new, timeless, and for the new to come into being, there cannot be any endeavor in the field in which effort is exercised as self-improvement or self-fulfillment. It is only when such effort totally ceases that the other is possible.

Please, this is really very important. It is not a question of gazing at your navel and going into some kind of illusion but of understanding the whole process of effort in society—this society of which you are the product, which you have built, and in which effort is essential because otherwise you are lost. If you are not ambitious, you are destroyed; if you are not acquisitive, you are trodden on; if you are not envious, you cannot be an executive or a big success. So you are constantly making effort to be or not to be, to become something, to be successful, to fulfill your ambition; and with that mentality, which is the product of society, you are trying to find something which is not of society.

Now, if one wishes to find that which is truth, one must be totally free from all religions, from all conditioning, from all dogmas, from all beliefs, from all authority which makes one conform, which means, essentially, standing completely alone, and that is very arduous; it is not a hobby for a Sunday morning when you go for a pleasant drive to sit under the trees and listen to some nonsense. To find out what is truth requires immense patience, gentleness, hesitancy. The mere studying of books has no value, but if as you listen you can be completely attentive, then you will see that this very attention frees you from effort so that without movement in any direction the mind is capable of receiving something which is extraordinarily beautiful and creative, something which is not to be measured by knowledge, by the past. It is only such a person who is really religious and revolutionary because he is no longer part of society. As long as one is ambitious, envious, acquisitive, competitive, one is society. With that mentality, which is extraordinarily difficult to be free of, one seeks God, and that search has no meaning at all because it is merely another endeavor to become something, to gain something. That is why it is very important to understand one's relationship to society, to be aware of all the beliefs, dogmas, tenets, superstitions that one has acquired, and to throw them off—not with effort, because then you will again be caught in it, but just to see these things for what they are and let them go, like the autumnal leaf that withers and is blown away, leaving the tree naked. It is only such a mind that can receive something which brings measureless happiness to life.

In discussing with you some of these questions, I am obviously not answering them because we are trying to find out together the significance of the question. If you are merely listening for an answer to the question, I'm afraid you will be disappointed because then you are not interested in the problem but are only concerned with the answer—as most of us are. I feel it is very important to ask fundamental questions and to keep on asking them without trying to find an answer, because the more you persist in asking fundamental questions, demanding, inquiring, the sharper and more aware the mind becomes. So what are the fundamental questions? Can anyone tell you what they are, or must you find out for yourself? If you can find out for yourself what are the fundamental questions, your mind has already altered; it has already become much more significant than when it asks a petty question and finds a petty answer.

Questioner: Juvenile delinquency in this country is increasing at an alarming rate. How is this mounting problem to be solved?

Krishnamurti: There is obviously revolt within the pattern of society. Some revolts are respectable, others are not, but they are always within the field of society, within the limits of the social fence. And surely, a society based on envy, on ambition, cruelty, war, must expect revolt within itself. After all, when you go to the cinema, the movies, you see a great deal of violence. There have been two enormous global wars, representing total violence. A nation which maintains an army must be destructive of its own citizens. Please listen to all this. No nation is peaceful as long as it has an army, whether it is a defensive or an offensive army. An army is both offensive and defensive; it does not bring about a peaceful state. The moment a culture establishes and maintains an army, it is destroying itself. This is historically a fact. And on every side we are encouraged to be competitive, to be ambitious, to be successful. Competition, ambition, and success are the gods of a particularly prosperous society such as this, and what do you expect? You want juvenile delinquency to become respectable, that's all. You do not tackle the roots of the problem, which is to stop this whole process of war, of maintaining an army, of being ambitious, of encouraging competition. These things, which are rooted in our hearts, are the fences of society within which there is revolt going on all the time on the part of both the young and the old. The problem is not only that of juvenile delinquency; it involves our whole social structure, and there is no answer to it as long as you and I do not step totally out of society—society representing ambition, cruelty, the desire to succeed, to become somebody, to be on top. That whole process is essentially the egocentric pursuit of fulfillment, only it has been made respectable. How you worship a successful man! How you decorate a man who kills thousands! And there are all the divisions of belief, of dogma—the Christian and the Hindu, the Buddhist and the Muslim. These are the things that are bringing about conflict; and when you seek to deal with juvenile delinquency by merely keeping the children at home, or disciplining them, or putting them in the army, or having recourse to the various solutions offered by every psychologist and social reformer, you are surely dealing very superficially with a fundamental question. But we are afraid to tackle fundamental questions because we would become unpopular, we would be termed communists or God knows what else, and labels seem to have extraordinary importance for most of us. Whether it is in Russia, in India, or here, the problem is essentially the same, and it is only when the mind understands this whole social structure that we shall find an entirely different approach to the problem, thereby perhaps establishing real peace, not this spurious peace of politicians.

Questioner: I have gone from teacher to teacher seeking, and now I have come to you in the same spirit of search. Are you any different from all the others, and how am I to know?

J. Krishnamurti

Krishnamurti: Now, you are really seeking, and what does it mean to seek? Do you understand the question? You are obviously seeking something, but what? Essentially, you are seeking a state of mind which will never be disturbed and which you call peace, God, love, or whatever it be. Is it not so? Our life is disturbed, anxious, full of fear, darkness, upheaval, confusion, and we want to escape from all that; but when a confused man seeks, his search is based on confusion, and therefore what he finds is further confusion. Are you following this?

First of all, then, we must inquire why we seek and what it is we are seeking. You may go from teacher to teacher, each teacher offering a different method of discipline or meditation, some foolish nonsense; so what is important, surely, is not the teacher and what he offers, but what it is you are seeking. If you can be very clear about what you are seeking, then you will find a teacher who will offer you that. If you are seeking peace, you will find a teacher who will offer you that which you seek. But that which you seek may not be true at all. Do you understand? I may want perfect bliss, which means an undisturbed state of mind in which there will be complete quietness, no conflict, no pain, no inquiry, no doubt; so I practice a discipline which some teacher offers, and probably that very discipline produces its own result, which I call peace. I might just as well take a drug, a pill, which will have the same effect—only that's not respectable, whereas the other is. [*Laughter*] Please, it is not a laughing matter; this is what we are actually doing.

So, that which you are seeking, you will find, obviously, if you are willing to pay for it. If you put yourself in the

28

hands of another, follow some authority, discipline, control yourself, you will find what you want, which means that your desire is dictating your search; but you are really not aware of the motivation of your search at all, and then you ask me what my position is and how you are to know whether what I am saying is true or false. Having gone to various teachers and been caught, burned, you now want to try this. But I am not telling you anything; actually I am not telling you anything at all. All that I am saying is to know yourself deeper and deeper, see yourself as you actually are, which nobody can teach you; and you cannot see yourself as you are if you are bound by beliefs, by dogmas, by superstitions, fears.

Sirs, for a mind that cannot stand alone, search will have no meaning at all. To stand alone is to be uncorrupted, innocent, free of all tradition, of dogma, of opinion, of what another says, and so on. Such a mind does not seek because there is nothing to seek; being free, such a mind is completely still without a want, without movement. But this state is not to be achieved; it isn't a thing that you buy through discipline; it doesn't come into being by giving up sex, or practicing a certain yoga. It comes into being only when there is understanding of the ways of the self, the 'me', which shows itself through the conscious mind in everyday activity, and also in the unconscious. What matters is to understand for oneself, not through the direction of others, the total content of consciousness, which is conditioned, which is the result of society, of religion, of various impacts, impressions, memories—to understand all that conditioning and be free of it. But there is no "how" to be free. If you ask how to be free, you are not listening.

Say, for example, I am telling you that the mind must be totally unconditioned. Now, how do you listen to a statement of that kind? With what attention are you listening to it? If you are watching your own mind, which I hope you are, you will see that you are inwardly saying, "How impossible this is," or "It cannot be done," or "Conditioning can only be modified," and so on. In other words, you are not listening to the statement attentively but you are opposing it with your own opinions, with your own conclusions, with your own knowledge; therefore, there is no attention.

The fact is that the mind is conditioned, whether as a communist, a Catholic, a Protestant, a Hindu, or whatever it be, and either we are unaware of this conditioning or we accept it or we try to modify it, ennoble it, change it; but we never put the question: Can the mind be totally free from conditioning? Before you can really put that question attentively to yourself, you must first be aware that your mind is conditioned, as it obviously is. Do you understand what I mean by conditioning? Not the superficial conditioning of language, gesture, costume, and all the rest of it, but conditioning in a much deeper, more fundamental sense. The mind is conditioned when it is ambitious, not only in this world, but ambitious to become something spiritual. This whole endeavor of self-improvement is the result of conditioning, and can the mind be totally free from such conditioning? If you really put that question to yourself, attentively, without seeking an answer, then you will find the right answer, which is not that it is possible or impossible, but something entirely different takes place.

Second Talk

So it is important to find out how we pay attention to these talks. If you don't pay attention, I assure you it is a waste of time for you to come here every weekend. It may be pleasant to drive to Ojai, but it's hot. Whereas, if you can pay direct attention to what is being said, which is not to remember something you have read, or to oppose opinion by opinion, or to take notes and say, "I'll think about it later," but actually to put the given question to yourself immediately, while you are listening, then that very actuality of attention brings about the right answer.

Questioner: It is now a well-established fact that many of our diseases are psychosomatic, brought on by deep inner frustrations and conflicts of which we are often unaware. Must we now run to psychiatrists as we used to run to physicians, or is there a way for man to free himself from this inner turmoil?

Krishnamurti: Which raises the question: What is the position of the psychoanalysts? And what is the position of those of us who have some form of disease or illness? Is the disease brought on by our emotional disturbances, or is it without emotional significance? Most of us are disturbed. Most of us are confused, in turmoil, even the very prosperous who have refrigerators, cars, and all the rest of it; and as we do not know how to deal with the disturbance, inevitably it reacts on the physical and produces an illness, which is fairly obvious. And the question is: Must we run to psychiatrists to help us to remove our disturbances and thereby regain health, or is it possible for us to find out for ourselves how not to be disturbed, how not to have turmoil, anxieties, fears?

Why are we disturbed, if we are? What is disturbance? I want something, but I can't get it, so I'm in a state. I want to fulfill through my children, through my wife, through my property, through position, success, and all the rest of it, but I am blocked, which means that I am disturbed. I am ambitious, but somebody else pushes me aside and gets ahead; again I am in chaos, in turmoil, which produces its own physical reaction.

Now, can you and I be free of all this turmoil and confusion? What is confusion? Do you understand? What is confusion? Confusion exists only when there is the fact plus what I think about the fact: my opinion about the fact, my disregard of the fact, my evasion of the fact, my evaluation of the fact, and so on. If I can look at the fact without the additive quality, then there is no confusion. If I recognize the fact that a certain road leads to Ventura, there is no confusion. Confusion arises only when I think or insist that the road leads somewhere else—and that is actually the state that most of us are in. Our opinions, our beliefs, our desires, ambitions, are so strong, we are so weighed down by them, that we are incapable of looking at the fact.

So, the fact plus opinion, judgment, evaluation, ambition, and all the rest of it, brings about confusion. And can you and I, being confused, not act? Surely, any action born of confusion must lead to further confusion, further turmoil, all of which reacts on the body, on the nervous system, and produces illness. Being confused, to acknowledge to oneself that one is confused requires, not courage, but a certain clarity of thought, clarity of perception. Most of us are afraid to acknowledge that we are confused, so out of our confusion we choose leaders, teachers, politicians; and when we choose something out of our confusion, that very choice must be confused, and therefore the leader must also be confused.

Is it possible, then, to be aware of our confusion, and to know the cause of that confusion, and not act? When a confused mind acts, it can only produce further confusion; but a mind that is aware that it is confused and understands this whole process of confusion need not act because that very clarity is its own action. I think this is rather difficult for most people to understand because we are so used to acting, doing; but if one can watch action, see what its results are, observe what is happening in the world politically and in every direction, then it becomes fairly obvious that so-called reformatory action is merely producing more confusion, more chaos, more reforms.

So can we individually be aware of our own confusion, of our own turmoil, and live with it, understand it, without wanting to get rid of it, push it away, or escape from it? As long as we are kicking it, condemning it, running away from it, that very condemnation, running away, is the process of confusion. And I do not think any analyst can solve this problem. He may temporarily help you to conform to a certain pattern of society which he calls normal existence, but the problem is much deeper than that, and no one can solve it except yourself. You and I have made this society; it is the result of our actions, of our thoughts, of our very being, and as long as we are merely trying to reform the product without understanding the entity that has produced it, we shall have more diseases, more chaos, more delinquency. The understanding of the self brings about wisdom and right action.

"Our problem is to be good without trying to be good. I think there is a vast difference between the two... A person who tries to be humble obviously has not the least understanding of what humility is. ... Is it possible to have the sense of humility without the cultivation of humility?"

I think one of our greatest difficulties is that of communication. I want to say something, naturally, with the intention that you should understand it, but each one of us interprets the words he hears according to his own peculiar background, and so with a large audience like this it is extremely difficult to convey exactly what one intends.

I would like to discuss this evening something that I consider quite important, and that is the whole problem of the cultivation of virtue. One can see that without virtue the mind is quite chaotic, contradictory, and without having a quiet, orderly mind in which there is no conflict, one obviously cannot go much further. But virtue is not an end in itself. The cultivation of virtue leads in one direction, and being virtuous leads in another. Most of us are concerned with the cultivation of virtue because, even though only superficially, virtue does give a certain poise, a certain quietness of mind in which there is not this incessant conflict of contradictory desires. But it seems to me fairly obvious that the mere cultivation of virtue can never bring about freedom, but only leads to respectable tranquillity, the sense of order, of control, which arises from shaping the mind to conform to a certain social pattern which is called virtue.

So, our problem is to be good without trying to be good. I think there is a vast difference between the two. Being good is a state in which there is no effort, but we are not in that state. We are envious, ambitious, gossipy, cruel, narrow, petty minded, caught in various forms of stupidity, which is not good; and being all that, how can one come to a state of mind which is good without making an effort to be good? Surely, the man who makes an effort to be virtuous is not virtuous, is he? A person who tries to be humble obviously has not the least understanding of what humility is. And not being humble, is it possible to have the sense of humility without the cultivation of humility?

I do not know if you have thought about this problem at all. One can see very well that there must be virtue. It is like keeping the room tidy, but having a tidy room is not at all important in itself. To make virtue an end in itself obviously has social benefits; it helps you to be a so-called decent citizen who lives according to a certain pattern, whether here, in India, or in Russia. But isn't it very important for the mind to be orderly without enforcement, without discipline, and to forget it so that it is not all the time restrained, disciplined, cultivating conformity?

After all, what is it we are seeking? What is it that each one of us is in search of, not theoretically, abstractly, but actually? And is there any difference between the search of the man who is seeking satisfaction through knowledge, through God, and that of the man who is seeking to be wealthy, to fulfill his ambition, or who seeks satisfaction through drink? Socially there is a difference. The man who is seeking satisfaction through drink is obviously an antisocial being, whereas the man who seeks satisfaction by joining a religious order, becoming a hermit, and so on, is socially beneficial—but that's all.

So, does what we are seeking actually bring about contentment, however serious we are in our search? And we are serious, are we not? The hermit, the monk, the man who is pursuing various forms of pleasure, each in his own way is very serious. And does that constitute earnestness? Is there earnestness when there is a search to acquire something? Do you understand my question? Or, is there earnestness only when there is no seeking of an end?

After all, you who are here must be somewhat earnest; otherwise, you wouldn't have taken the trouble to come. Now, I am asking myself, and I hope you are asking yourself, what it means to be earnest because on that depends, I think, what I am going to explain a little later. If you are here seeking contentment, or to understand some past experience, or to cultivate a certain state of mind which you think will give you tranquillity, peace, or to experience that which you call reality, God, you may be very earnest; but should you not question that earnestness? Is it earnestness when you are seeking something which is going to give you pleasure or tranquillity?

If we can really understand this whole process of seeking, understand why we seek and what we seek—and that process can be understood only through self-knowledge, through awareness of the movement of our own thinking, of our own reactions and responses, of our various urges—then perhaps we shall find out what it is to be virtuous without disciplining ourselves to be virtuous. You see, I feel that as long as the mind is held in conflict, though we may suppress it, though we may try to run away from it, discipline it, control it, shape it according to various patterns, that conflict remains latent in the mind, and such a mind can never be really quiet. And it is essential, it seems to me, to have a quiet mind because the mind is our only instrument of understanding, of perception, of communication, and as long as that instrument is not completely clear and capable of perception, capable of pursuit without an end, there can be no freedom, no tranquillity, and therefore no discovery of anything new.

So, is it possible to live in this world—where there is so much turmoil, anxiety, insecurity—without effort? That is one of our problems, is it not? To me, that is a very important question because creativity is something that comes into being only when the mind is in a state of no effort. I am not using that word *creativity* in the academic sense of learning creative writing, creative acting, creative thought, and all that stuff; I am using it in an entirely different sense. When the mind is in a state where the past, with its cultivation of virtue through discipline, has wholly ceased—it is only then that there is a timeless creativity, which may be called God, truth, or what you like. So, how can the mind be in that state of constant creativity?

When you have a problem, what happens? You think it out, you wallow in it, you fuss over it, you get wildly excited about it; and the more you analyze it, dig into it, polish it, worry about it, the less you understand it. But the moment you put it away from you, you understand it—the whole thing is suddenly very clear. I think most of us have had that experience. The mind is no longer in a state of confusion, conflict, and therefore it is capable of receiving or perceiving something totally new. And is it possible for the mind to be in that state so that it is never repetitive but is experiencing something new all the time? I think that depends on our understanding of this problem of the cultivation of virtue.

We cultivate virtue; we discipline ourselves to conform to a particular pattern of morality. Why? Not only in order to be socially respectable, but also because we see the necessity of bringing about order, of controlling our minds, our speech, our thought. We see how extraordinarily important that is, but in the process of cultivating virtue, we are building up memory, the memory which is the 'me', the self, the ego. That is the background we have, especially those who think they are religious—the background of constantly practicing a particular discipline, of belonging to certain sects, groups, so-called religious bodies. Their reward may be somewhere else, in the next world, but it is still a reward; and in pursuing virtue, which means polishing, disciplining, controlling the mind, they are developing and maintaining self-conscious memory, so never for a moment are they free from the past.

If you have ever really disciplined yourself, practiced not being envious, not being angry, and so on, I wonder if you have noticed that that very practice, the very disciplining of the mind, leaves a series of memories of the known? This is rather a difficult problem we are discussing, and I hope I am making myself clear. The whole process of saying, "I must not do this," breeds or builds up time, and a mind that is caught in time can obviously never experience something which is timeless, which is the unknown. Yet the mind must be orderly, free of contradictory desires—which does not mean conforming, accepting, obeying.

So, if you are at all earnest, in the sense in which I am using that word, this problem must inevitably arise. Your mind is the result of the known. Your mind is the known; it is shaped by memories, by reactions, by impressions of the known; and a mind that is held within the field of the known can never comprehend or experience the unknown, something which is not within the field of time. The mind is creative only when it is free from the known—and then it can use the known, which is the technique. Am I making myself clear, or is it all as clear as mud? [*Laughter*]

You see, we are so bored that we constantly read, acquire, learn, go to churches, perform rituals, and we never know a moment which is original, pristine, innocent, completely free from all impressions; and it is that moment that is creative, that is timeless, everlasting, or whatever word you like to use. Without that creativity, life becomes so insipid, stupid, and then all our virtues, our knowledge, our pursuits, our amusements, our various beliefs and traditions have very little meaning. As I was saying the other day, society merely cultivates the known, and we are the result of that society. To find the unknown, it is essential to be free of society—which doesn't mean that you must withdraw into a monastery and pray from morning till night, everlastingly disciplining yourself, conforming to a certain belief, dogma. Surely, that does not bring about the release of the mind from the known.

The mind is the result of the known; it is the result of the past, which is the accumulation of time; and is it possible for such a mind to be free from the known without effort so that it can discover something original? Any effort it makes to free itself, any search in order to find, is still within the field of the known. Surely, God or truth must be something totally unthought of; it must be something entirely new, unformulated, never discovered, never experienced before. And how can a mind which is the result of the known ever experience that? Do you follow the problem? If the problem is clear, then you will find the right way of approaching it, which is not a method.

That's why it is important to find out if one can be good, in the complete sense of the word, without trying to be good, without making an effort to get rid of envy, of ambition, of cruelty, without disciplining oneself to stop gossiping—you know, the whole mass of strictures which we impose upon ourselves in order to be good. Can there be goodness without the attempt to be good? I think there can be only if each one of us knows how to listen, how to be attentive—now. There is goodness only when there is complete attention. See the truth that there can be no goodness through endeavor, through effort, just see the truth of that—and you can see the truth of it only if you are giving complete attention to what is being said. Forget all the books you have read, the things that you have been told of, and give complete attention to the statement that there can be no virtue as long as there is endeavor to be virtuous. As long as I am trying to be nonviolent, there is violence; as long as I am trying to be unenvious, I am envious; as long as I am trying to be humble, there is pride. If I see the truth of that, not intellectually or verbally, which is merely to hear the words and agree with them, but very simply and directly, then out of that comes goodness. But the difficulty is that the mind then says, "How can I keep that state? I may be good while sitting here listening to something which I feel is true, but the moment I go out, I am again caught in the stream of envy." But I don't think that matters—you'll find out.

Our culture, our society, is based on envy, on various forms of acquisitiveness, whether it is the acquisition of knowledge, of experience, of property, or what you will. And to be free of all that doesn't require endeavor, effort, but seeing the whole implication of effort. A man who is acquiring knowledge is not peaceful, he is caught in effort. It is only when the mind is totally without effort that it is peaceful, which is really an extraordinary state, and I think anybody can have it who gives his heart, his whole attention, to the matter. A mind that is not toiling, that is not trying to become something socially or spiritually, that is completely nothing—it is only such a mind that can receive the new.

Questioner: Some philosophers assert that life has purpose and meaning while others maintain that life is utterly haphazard and absurd. What do you say? You deny the value of goals, ideals, and purposes; but without them, has life any significance at all?

Krishnamurti: Has what the philosophers say a great significance to each one of us? Some intellectuals say there is meaning, significance to life, while others say it is haphazard and absurd. Surely, in their own way, negatively or positively, both are giving significance to life, are they not? One asserts, the other denies, but essentially they are both the same. That is fairly obvious.

Now, when you pursue an ideal, a goal, or inquire what is the purpose of life, that very inquiry or pursuit is based on the desire to give significance to life, is it not? I do not know if you are following all this.

My life has no significance, let us suppose, so I seek to give significance to life. I say, "What is the purpose of life?" because if life has a purpose, then according to that purpose, I can live. So I invent or imagine a purpose, or by reading, inquiring, searching, I find a purpose; therefore, I am giving significance to life. As the intellectual in his own way gives significance to life by denying or asserting that it has purpose and meaning, we also give significance to life through our ideals, through our search for a goal, for God, for love, for truth. Which means, really, that without giving significance to life, our life has no meaning for us at all. Living isn't good enough for us, so we want to give a significance to life. I do not know if you see that.

What is the significance of our life, yours and mine, apart from the philosophers? Has it any significance, or are we giving it a significance through belief, like the intellectual who becomes a Catholic, this or that, and thereby finds shelter? His intellect has torn everything to pieces; he cannot stand being alone, lonely, and all the rest of it, so he has to have a belief in Catholicism, in communism, or in something else which nourishes him, which for him gives significance to life.

Now, I am asking myself: Why do we want a significance? And what does it mean to live without significance at all? Do you understand? Our own life being empty, harried, lonely, we want to give a significance to life. And is it possible to be aware of our own emptiness, loneliness, sorrow, of all the travail and conflict in our life, without trying to get out of it, without artificially giving a significance to life? Can we be aware of this extraordinary thing which we call life, which is the earning of a livelihood, the envy, the ambition, the frustration—just be aware of all that without condemnation or justification, and go beyond? It seems to me that as long as we are seeking or giving a significance to life, we are missing something extraordinarily vital. It is like the man who wants to find the significance of death, who is everlastingly rationalizing it, explaining it—he never experiences what is death. We shall go into that in another talk.

So, aren't we all trying to find a reason for our existence? When we love, do we have a reason? Or is love the only state in which there is no reason at all, no explanation, no endeavor, no trying to be something? Perhaps we do not know that state. Not knowing that state, we try to imagine it, give significance to life; and because our minds are conditioned, limited, petty, the significance we give to life, our gods, our rituals, our endeavors, is also petty.

Isn't it important, then, to find out for ourselves what significance we give to life, if we do? Surely, the purposes, the goals, the Masters, the gods, the beliefs, the ends through which we are seeking fulfillment are all invented by the mind; they are all the outcome of our conditioning, and realizing that, is it not important to uncondition the mind? When the mind is unconditioned and is therefore not giving significance to life, then life is an extraordinary thing, something totally different from the framework of the mind. But first we must know our own conditioning, must we not? And is it possible to know our conditioning, our limitations, our background, without forcing, without analyzing, without trying to sublimate or suppress it? Because that whole process involves the entity who observes and separates himself from the observed, does it not? As long as there is the observer and the observed, conditioning must continue. However much the observer, the thinker, the censor, may try to get rid of his conditioning, he is still caught in that conditioning because the very division between the thinker and the thought, the experiencer and the experience, is the perpetuation of conditioning; and it is extremely difficult to let this division disappear because it involves the whole problem of will.

Our culture is based on will—the will to be, to become, to achieve, to fulfill—therefore, in each one of us there is always the entity who is trying to change, control, alter that which he observes. But is there a difference between that which he observes and himself, or are they one? This is a thing that cannot be merely accepted. It must be thought of, gone into with tremendous patience, gentleness, hesitancy, so that the mind is no longer separated from that which it thinks, so that the observer and the observed are psychologically one. As long as I am psychologically separate from that which I perceive in myself as envy, I try to overcome envy; but is that 'I', the maker of effort to overcome envy, different from envy? Or are they both the same, only the 'I' has separated himself from envy in order to overcome it because he feels envy is painful, and for various other reasons? But that very separation is the cause of envy.

Perhaps you are not used to this way of thinking, and it is a little bit too abstract. But a mind that is envious can never be tranquil because it is always comparing, always trying to become something which it is not; and if one really goes into this problem of envy radically, profoundly, deeply, one must inevitably come upon this problem—whether the entity that wishes to be rid of envy is not envy itself. When one realizes that it is envy itself that wants to get rid of envy, then the mind is aware of that feeling called envy without any sense of condemning or trying to get rid of it. Then from that the problem arises: Is there a feeling if there is no verbalization? Because the very word envy is condemnatory, is it not? Am I saying too much all at once?

Is there a feeling of envy if I don't name that feeling? By the very naming of it, am I not maintaining that feeling? The feeling and the naming are almost simultaneous, are they not? And is it possible to separate them so that there is only a sense of reaction without naming? If you really go into it, you will find that when there is no naming of that feeling, envy totally ceases—not just the envy you feel because somebody is more beautiful or has a better car, and all that stupid stuff, but the tremendous depth of envy, the root of envy. All of us are envious; there isn't one who is not envious in different ways. But envy isn't just the superficial thing; it is the whole sense of comparing which goes very deep and occupies our minds so vastly, and to be radically free of envy, there must be no censor, no observer of the envy who is trying to get rid of envy. We shall go into that another time.

Third Talk

Questioner: To be without condemnation, justification, or comparison is to be in a higher state of consciousness. I am not in that state, so how am I to get there?

Krishnamurti: You see, the very question, "How am I to get there?" is envious. [*Laughter*] No, sirs, please pay attention. You want to get something, so you have methods, disciplines, religions, churches, this whole superstructure which is built on envy, comparison, justification, condemnation. Our culture is based on this hierarchical division between those who have more and those who have less, those who know and those who don't know, those who are ignorant and those who are full of wisdom, so our approach to the problem is totally wrong. The questioner says, "To be without condemnation, justification, or comparison is to be in a higher state of consciousness." Is it? Or are we simply not aware that we are condemning, comparing? Why do we first assert that it is a higher state of consciousness and then out of that create the problem of how to get there and who is going to help us to get there? Is it not much simpler than all that?

That is, we are not aware of ourselves at all; we do not see that we are condemning, comparing. If we can watch ourselves daily without justifying or condemning anything, just be aware of how we never think without judging, comparing, evaluating, then that very awareness is enough. We are always saying, "This book is not as good as the other," or "This man is better than that man," and so on; there is this constant process of comparison, and we think that through comparison we understand. Do we? Or does understanding come only when one is not comparing but is really paying attention? Is there comparison when you are looking attentively at something? When you are totally attentive, you have no time to compare, have you? The moment you compare, your attention has gone off to something else. When you say, "This sunset is not as beautiful as that of yesterday," you are not really looking at the sunset; your mind has already gone off to yesterday's memory. But if you can look at the sunset completely, totally, with your whole attention, then comparison ceases, surely.

So the problem is not how to get something but why we are not attentive. We are not attentive, obviously, because we are not interested. Don't say, "How am I to be interested?" That's irrelevant, that's not the question. Why should you be interested? If you are not interested in listening to what is being said, why bother? But you are bothered because your life is full of envy, suffering, so you want to find an answer, you want to find a meaning. If you want to find a meaning, give full attention. The difficulty is that we are not really serious about anything, serious in the right sense of that word. When you give complete attention to something, you are not trying to get anything out of it, are you? At that moment of total attention, there is no entity who is trying to change, to modify, to become something; there is no self at all. In the moment of attention the self, the 'me', is absent, and it is that moment of attention that is good, that is love.

"If we want to understand the problem of sorrow and perhaps put an end to it, then we cannot possibly think in terms of progress because a man who thinks in terms of progress, of time, saying that he will be happy tomorrow, is living in sorrow."

"Self-improvement is progress in sorrow, not the cessation of sorrow."

One of the most difficult things to understand, it seems to me, is this problem of change. We see that there is progress in different forms, so-called evolution, but is there a fundamental change in progress? I do not know if this problem has struck you at all, or whether you have ever thought about it, but perhaps it will be worthwhile to go into the question this morning.

We see that there is progress in the obvious sense of that word; there are new inventions, better cars, better planes, better refrigerators, the superficial peace of a progressive society, and so on. But does that progress bring about a radical change in man, in you and me? It does superficially alter the conduct of our life, but can it ever fundamentally transform our thinking? And how is this fundamental transformation to be brought about? I think it is a problem worth considering. There is progress in self-improvement—I can be better tomorrow, more kind, more generous, less envious, less ambitious. But does self-improvement bring about a complete change in one's thinking? Or is there no change at all, but only progress? Progress implies time, does it not? I am this today, and I shall be something better tomorrow. That is, in self-improvement or self-denial or self-abnegation, there is progression, the gradualism of moving towards a better life, which means superficially adjusting to environment,

J. Krishnamurti

conforming to an improved pattern, being conditioned in a nobler way, and so on. We see that process taking place all the time. And you must have wondered, as I have, whether progress does bring about a fundamental revolution.

To me, the important thing is not progress but revolution. Please don't be horrified by that word *revolution*, as most people are in a very progressive society like this. But it seems to me that unless we understand the extraordinary necessity of bringing about not just a social amelioration but a radical change in our outlook, mere progress is progress in sorrow; it may effect the pacification, the calming of sorrow, but not the cessation of sorrow, which is always latent. After all, progress in the sense of getting better over a period of time is really the process of the self, the 'me', the ego. There is progress in self-improvement, obviously, which is the determined effort to be good, to be more this or less that, and so on. As there is improvement in refrigerators and airplanes, so also there is improvement in the self, but that improvement, that progress, does not free the mind from sorrow.

So, if we want to understand the problem of sorrow and perhaps put an end to it, then we cannot possibly think in terms of progress because a man who thinks in terms of progress, of time, saying that he will be happy tomorrow, is living in sorrow. And to understand this problem, one must go into the whole question of consciousness, must one not? Is this too difficult a subject? I'll go on and we'll see.

If I really want to understand sorrow and the ending of sorrow, I must find out, not only what are the implications of progress, but also what that entity is who wants to improve himself, and I must also know the motive with which he seeks to improve. All this is consciousness. There is the superficial consciousness of everyday activity: the job, the family, the constant adjustment to social environment, either happily, easily, or contradictorily, with a neurosis. And there is also the deeper level of consciousness, which is the vast social inheritance of man through centuries: the will to exist, the will to alter, the will to become. If I would bring about a fundamental revolution in myself, surely I must understand this total progress of consciousness.

One can see that progress obviously does not bring about a revolution. I am not talking of social or economic revolution—that is very superficial, as I think most of us will agree. The overthrow of one economic or social system and the setting up of another does alter certain values, as in the Russian and other historical revolutions. But I am talking of a psychological revolution, which is the only revolution, and a man who is religious must be in that state of revolution, which I shall go into presently.

In grappling with this problem of progress and revolution, there must be an awareness, a comprehension of the total process of consciousness. Do you understand? Until I really comprehend what is consciousness, mere adjustment on the surface, though it may have sociological significance and perhaps bring about a better way of living, more food, less starvation in Asia, fewer wars, can never solve the fundamental problem of sorrow. Without understanding, resolving, and going beyond the urge that brings about sorrow, mere social adjustment is the continuance of that latent seed of sorrow. So I must understand what is consciousness, not according to any philosophy, psychology, or description, but by directly experiencing the actual state of my consciousness, the whole content of it.

Now, perhaps this morning you and I can experiment with this. I am going to describe what is consciousness; but while I am describing it, don't follow the description, but rather observe the process of your own thinking, and then you will know for yourself what consciousness is without reading any of the contradictory accounts of what the various experts have found. Do you understand? I am describing something. If you merely listen to the description, it will have very little meaning; but if through the description you are experiencing your own consciousness, your own process of thinking, then it will have tremendous importance now, not tomorrow, not some other day when you will have time to think about it, which is absolutely nonsense because it is mere postponement. If through the description you can experience the actual state of your own consciousness as you are quietly sitting here, then you will find that the mind is capable of freeing itself from its vast inheritance of conditioning, all the accumulations and edicts of society, and is able to go beyond self-consciousness. So if you will experiment with this, it will be worthwhile.

We are trying to discover for ourselves what is consciousness, and whether it is possible for the mind to be free of sorrow—not to change the pattern of sorrow, not to decorate the prison of sorrow, but to be completely free from the seed, the root of sorrow. In inquiring into that, we shall see the difference between progress and the psychological revolution which is essential if there is to be freedom from sorrow. We are not trying to alter the conduct of our consciousness; we are not trying to do something about it; we are just looking at it. Surely, if we are at all observant, slightly aware of anything, we know the activities of the superficial consciousness. We can see that on the surface our mind is active, occupied in adjustment, in a job, in earning a livelihood, in expressing certain tendencies, gifts, talents, or acquiring certain technical knowledge; and most of us are satisfied to live on that surface.

Please do not merely follow what I am telling you, but watch yourself, your own way of thinking. I am describing what is superficially taking place in our daily life—distractions, escapes, occasional lapses into fear, adjustment to the wife, to the husband, to the family, to society, to tradition, and so on—and with that superficiality most of us are satisfied.

Now, can we go below that and see the motive of this superficial adjustment? Again, if you are a little aware of this whole process, you know that this adjustment to opinion, to values, this acceptance of authority, and so on, is motivated by self-perpetuation, self-protection. If you can go still below that, you will find there is this vast undercurrent of racial, national, and group instincts, all the accumulations of human struggle, knowledge, endeavor, the dogmas and traditions of the Hindu, the Buddhist, or the Christian, the residue of so-called education through centuries—all of which has conditioned the mind to a certain inherited pattern. And if you can go deeper still, there is the primal desire to be, to succeed, to become, which expresses itself on the surface in various forms of social activity and creates deep-rooted anxieties, fears. Put very succinctly, the whole of that is our consciousness. In other words, our thinking is based on this fundamental urge to be, to become, and on top of that lie the many layers of tradition, of culture, of education, and the superficial conditioning of a given society—all forcing us to conform to a pattern that enables us to survive. There are many details and subtleties, but in essence that is our consciousness.

Now, any progress within that consciousness is self-improvement, and self-improvement is progress in sorrow, not the cessation of sorrow. This is quite obvious if you look at it. And if the mind is concerned with being free of all sorrow, then what is the mind to do? I do not know if you have thought about this problem, but please think about it now.

We suffer, don't we? We suffer, not only from physical illness, disease, but also from loneliness, from the poverty of our being; we suffer because we are not loved. When we love somebody and there is no loving in return, there is sorrow. In every direction, to think is to be full of sorrow; therefore, it seems better not to think, so we accept a belief and stagnate in that belief, which we call religion.

Now, if the mind sees that there is no ending of sorrow through self-improvement, through progress, which is fairly obvious, then what is the mind to do? Can the mind go beyond this consciousness, beyond these various urges and contradictory desires? And is going beyond a matter of time? Please follow this, not merely verbally, but actually. If it is a matter of time, then you are back again in the other thing, which is progress. Do you see that? Within the framework of consciousness, any movement in any direction is self-improvement and therefore the continuance of sorrow. Sorrow may be controlled, disciplined, subjugated, rationalized, super-refined, but the potential quality of sorrow is still there; and to be free from sorrow, there must be freedom from this potentiality, from this seed of the 'I', the self, from the whole process of becoming. To go beyond, there must be the cessation of this process. But if you say, "How am I to go beyond?" then the "how" becomes the method, the practice, which is still progress, therefore there is no going beyond but only the refinement of consciousness in sorrow. I hope you are getting this.

The mind thinks in terms of progress, of improvement, of time; and is it possible for such a mind, seeing that so-called progress is progress in sorrow, to come to an end—not in time, not tomorrow, but immediately? Otherwise you are back again in the whole routine, in the old wheel of sorrow. If the problem is stated clearly and clearly understood, then you will find the absolute answer. I am using that word *absolute* in its right sense. There is no other answer.

That is, our consciousness is all the time struggling to adjust, to modify, to change, to absorb, to reject, to evaluate, to condemn, to justify; but any such movement of consciousness is still within the pattern of sorrow. Any movement within that consciousness as dreams, or as an exertion of will, is the movement of the self; and any movement of the self, whether towards the highest or towards the most mundane, breeds sorrow. When the mind sees that, then what happens to such a mind? Do you understand the question? When the mind sees the truth of that, not merely verbally but totally, then is there a problem? Is there a problem when I am watching a rattler and know it to be poisonous? Similarly, if I can give my total attention to this process of suffering, then is not the mind beyond suffering?

Please follow this. Our minds are now occupied with sorrow and with the avoidance of sorrow, trying to overcome it, to diminish it, to modify it, to refine it, to run away from it in various ways. But if I see, not just superficially, but right through, that this very occupation of the mind with sorrow is the movement of the self which creates sorrow—if I really see the truth of that, then has not the mind gone beyond this thing that we call self-consciousness?

To put it differently, our society is based on envy, on acquisitiveness, not only here in America, but also in Europe, in Asia; and we are the product of that society, which has existed for centuries, millennia. Now, please follow this. I realize that I am envious. I can refine it, I can control it, discipline it, find a substitute for it through charitable activities, social reform, and so on; but envy is always there, latent, ready to spring forward. So, how is the mind to be totally free from envy? Because envy inevitably brings conflict, envy is a state in which there is no creativity, and a man who wishes to find out what is creativity must obviously be free from all envy, from all comparison, from the urges to be, to become.

Envy is a feeling which we identify with a word. We identify the feeling by calling it a name, giving it the term *envy*. I shall go slowly, and please follow this, for it is the description of our consciousness. There is a state of feeling, and I give it a name, I call it *envy*. That very word *envy* is condemnatory; it has social, moral, and spiritual significances which are part of the tradition in which I have been educated, so by the very employment of that word, I have condemned the feeling, and this process of condemnation is self-improvement. In condemning envy, I am progressing in the opposite direction, which is nonenvy, but that movement is still from the center which is envious.

So, can the mind put an end to naming? When there is a feeling of jealousy, of lust, or of ambition to be something, can the mind, which is educated in words, in condemnation, in giving it a name, stop that whole process of naming? Experiment with this, and you will see how extraordinarily difficult it is not to name a feeling. The feeling and the naming are almost simultaneous. But if the naming does not take place, then is there the feeling? Does the feeling persist when there is no naming? Are you following all this, or is it too abstract? Don't agree or disagree with me, because this is not my life, it is your life.

This whole problem of naming a feeling, of giving it a term, is part of the problem of consciousness. Take a word like *love*. How immediately your mind rejoices in that word! It has such significance, such beauty, ease, and all the rest of it. And the word *hate* immediately has quite another significance, something to be avoided, to be got rid of, to be shunned, and so on. So words have an extraordinary psychological effect on the mind, whether we are conscious of it or not.

Now, can the mind be free from all that verbalizing? If it can—and it must, otherwise the mind cannot possibly go further—then the problem arises: Is there an experiencer apart from experience? If there is an experiencer apart from experience, then the mind is conditioned because the experiencer is always either accumulating or rejecting experience, translating every experience in terms of his own likes and dislikes, in terms of his background, his conditioning; if he has a vision, he thinks it is Jesus, a Master, or God knows what else, some stupid nonsense. So as long as there is an experiencer, there is progress in suffering, which is the process of self-consciousness.

Now, to go beyond, to transcend all that, requires tremendous attention. This total attention, in which there is no choice, no sense of becoming, of changing, altering, wholly frees the mind from the process of self-consciousness; there is then no experiencer who is accumulating, and it is only then that the mind can be truly said to be free from sorrow. It is accumulation that is the cause of sorrow. We do not die to everything from day to day; we do not die to the innumerable traditions, to the family, to our own experiences, to our own desire to hurt another. One has to die to all that from moment to moment, to that vast accumulative memory, and only then the mind is free from the self, which is the entity of accumulation.

Perhaps in considering this question together, we shall clarify what has already been said.

Questioner: What is the unconscious, and is it conditioned? If it is conditioned, then how is one to set about being free from that conditioning?

Krishnamurti: First of all, is not our consciousness, the waking consciousness, conditioned? Do you understand what the word *conditioned* means? You are educated in a certain way. Here in this country you are conditioned to be Americans, whatever that may mean, you are educated in the American way of life, and in Russia they are educated in the Russian way of life. In Italy the Catholics educate the children to think in a certain way, which is another form of conditioning, while in India, in Asia, in the Buddhist countries, they are conditioned in still other ways. Throughout the world there is this deliberate process of conditioning the mind through education, through social environment, through fear, through the job, through the family—you know, the innumerable ways of influencing the superficial mind, the waking consciousness.

Then there is the unconscious, that is, the layer of the mind below the superficial, and the questioner wants to know if that is conditioned. Isn't it conditioned—conditioned by all the racial thought, the hidden motives, desires, the instinctual responses of a particular culture? I am supposed to be a Hindu, born in India, educated abroad, and all the rest of it. Until I go into the unconscious and understand it, I am still a Hindu with all the Brahmanic, symbolic, cultural, religious, superstitious responses—it is all there, dormant, to be awakened at any moment, and it gives warning, intimation, through dreams, through moments when the conscious mind is not fully occupied. So the unconscious is also conditioned.

It is quite obvious, then, if you go into it, that the whole of one's consciousness is conditioned. There is no part of you, no higher self, which is not conditioned. Your very thinking is the outcome of memory, conscious or unconscious; therefore, it is the result of conditioning. You think as a communist, as a socialist, as a capitalist, as an American, as a Hindu, as a Catholic, as a Protestant, or what you will, because you are conditioned that way. You are conditioned to believe in God, if you are, and the communist is not; he laughs at you and says, "You are conditioned," but he himself is conditioned, educated by his society, by the party to which he belongs, by its literature, not to believe. So we are all conditioned, and we never ask, "Is it possible to be totally free from conditioning?" All we know is a process of refinement in conditioning, which is refinement in sorrow.

Now, if I see that, not merely verbally, but with total attention, then there is no conflict. Do you understand what I mean? When you attend to something with your whole being, that is, when you give your mind completely to understand something, there is no conflict. Conflict arises only when you are partly interested and partly looking at something else, and then you want to overcome that conflict, so you begin to concentrate, which is not attention. In attention there is no division, there is no distraction; therefore, there is no effort, no conflict, and it is only through such attention that there can be self-knowledge, which is not accumulative.

Please follow this. Self-knowledge is not a thing to be accumulated; it is to be discovered from moment to moment, and to discover there cannot be accumulation, there cannot be a referent. If you accumulate self-knowledge, then all further understanding is dictated by that accumulation; therefore, there is no understanding.

So the mind can go beyond all conditioning only in awareness in which there is total attention. In that total attention there is no modifier, no censor, no entity who says, "I must change," which means there is a complete cessation of the experiencer. There is no experiencer as the accumulator. Please, this is really important to understand. Because, after all, when we experience something lovely—a sunset, a single leaf dancing in a tree, moonlight on the water, a smile, a vision, or what you like—the mind immediately wants to grasp it, to hold it, to worship it, which means the repetition of that experience; and where there is the urge to repeat, there must be sorrow.

Is it possible, then, to be in a state of experiencing without the experiencer? Do you understand? Can the mind experience ugliness, beauty, or what you will, without the entity who says, "I have experienced"? Because that which is truth, that which is God, that which is the immeasurable, can never be experienced as long as there is an experiencer. The experiencer is the entity of recognition; and if I am capable of recognizing that which is truth, then I have already experienced it, I already know it; therefore, it is not truth. That is the beauty of truth; it remains timelessly the unknown, and a mind that is the result of the known can never grasp it.

Questioner: You have said that all urges are in essence the same. Do you mean to say that the urge of the man who pursues God is no different from the urge of the man who pursues women or who loses himself in drink?

Krishnamurti: All urges are not similar, but they are all urges. You may have an urge towards God, and I may have an urge to get drunk, but we are both compelled, urged—you in one direction, I in another. Your direction is respectable, mine is not; on the contrary, I am antisocial. But the hermit, the monk, the so-called religious person whose mind is occupied with virtue, with God, is essentially the same as the man whose mind is occupied with business, with women, or with drink, because both are occupied. Do you understand? The one has sociological value, while the other, the man whose mind is occupied with drink, is socially unfit. So you are judging from the social point of view, are you not? The man who retires into a monastery and prays from morning till night, doing some gardening for a certain period of the day, whose mind is wholly occupied with God, with self-castigation, self-discipline, self-control—him you regard as a very holy person, a most extraordinary man. Whereas, the man who goes after business, who manipulates the stock exchange and is occupied all the time with making money, of him you say, "Well, he is just an ordinary man like the rest of us." But they are both occupied. To me, what the mind is occupied with is not important. A man whose mind is occupied with God will never find God because God is not something to be occupied with; it is the unknown, the immeasurable. You cannot occupy yourself with God. That is a cheap way of thinking of God.

What is significant is not with what the mind is occupied but the fact of its occupation, whether it be with the kitchen, with the children, with amusement, with what kind of food you are going to have, or with virtue, with God. And must the mind be occupied? Do you follow? Can an occupied mind ever see anything new, anything except its own occupation? And what happens to the mind if it is not occupied? Do you understand? Is there a mind if there is no occupation? The scientist is occupied with his technical problems, with his mechanics, with his mathematics, as the housewife is occupied in the kitchen or with the baby. We are all so frightened of not being occupied, frightened of the social implications. If one were not occupied, one might discover oneself as one is, so occupation becomes an escape from what one is.

So, must the mind be everlastingly occupied? And is it possible to have no occupation of the mind? Please, I am putting to you a question to which there is no answer because you have to find out, and when you do find out, you will see the extraordinary thing happen.

It is very interesting to find out for yourself how your mind is occupied. The artist is occupied with his art, with his name, with his progress, with the mixing of colors, with fame, with notoriety; the man of knowledge is occupied with his knowledge; and a man who is pursuing self-knowledge is occupied with his self-knowledge, trying like a little ant to be aware of every thought, every movement. They are all the same. It is only the mind that is totally unoccupied, completely empty—it is only such a mind that can receive something new, in which there is no occupation. But that new thing cannot come into being as long as the mind is occupied.

Questioner: You say that an occupied mind cannot receive that which is truth or God. But how can I earn a livelihood unless I am occupied with my work? Are you yourself not occupied with these talks, which is your particular means of earning a livelihood?

Krishnamurti: God forbid that I should be occupied with my talks! I am not. And this is not my means of livelihood. If I were occupied, there would be no interval between thoughts, there would not be that silence which is essential to see something new. Then talking would become utter boredom. I don't want to be bored by my own talks; therefore, I am not talking from memory. It is something totally different. It doesn't matter; we shall go into that some other time.

The questioner asks how he is to earn his livelihood if he is not occupied with his work. Do you occupy yourself with your work? Please listen to this. If you are occupied with your work, then you do not love your work. Do you understand the difference? If I love what I am doing, I am not occupied with it, my work is not apart from me. But we are trained in this country, and unfortunately it is becoming the habit throughout the world to acquire skill in work which we don't love. There may be a few scientists, a few technical experts, a few engineers who really love what they do in the total sense of the word, which I am going to explain presently. But most of us do not love what we are doing and that is why we are occupied with our livelihood. I think there is a difference between the two if you really go into it. How can I love what I am doing if I am all the time driven by ambition, trying through my work to achieve an aim, to become somebody, to have a success? An artist who is concerned with his name, with his greatness, with comparison, with fulfilling his ambition, has ceased to be an artist; he is merely a technician like everybody else. Which means, really, that to love something there must be a total cessation of all ambition, of all desire for the recognition of society, which is rotten anyhow. [Laughter] Sirs, please don't. And we are not trained for that, we are not educated for that; we have to fit into some groove which society or the family has given us. Because my forefathers have been doctors, lawyers, or engineers, I must be a doctor, a lawyer, or an engineer. And now there must be more and more engineers because that is what society demands. So we have lost this love of the thing itself, if we ever had it, which I doubt. And when you love a thing, there is no occupation with it. The mind isn't conniving to achieve something, trying to be better than somebody else; all comparison, competition, all desire for success, for fulfillment, totally ceases. It is only the ambitious mind that is occupied.

Similarly, a mind that is occupied with God, with truth, can never find it because that which the mind is occupied with, it already knows. If you already know the immeasurable, what you know is the outcome of the past; therefore, it is not the immeasurable. Reality cannot be measured; therefore, there is no occupation with it; there is only a stillness of the mind, an emptiness in which there is no movement—and it is only then that the unknown can come into being.

"Cultures create religions but not the religious man. The religious man comes into being only when the mind rejects culture, which is the background, and is therefore free to find out what is true. ... Such a person is not an American, an Englishman, or a Hindu but a human being; he does not belong to any particular group, race, or culture and is therefore free to find out what is true, what is God. No culture helps man to find out what is true. Cultures only create organizations which bind man."

One of the grave problems about which most of us must have thought is the complete control of the mind, because one can see that without a deep, rational, balanced control of the mind, there is not the conservation of energy which is so essential if one is to do anything, and especially in matters that pertain to so-called search—the search of truth, of reality, of God, or what you will. One is aware, I think, that this stability of mind is necessary to penetrate into fundamental problems, which a superficial mind cannot touch. And yet the difficulty lies in how to control the mind, does it not? Many systems of discipline, various religious sects and monastic communities, have always insisted on the absolute control of the mind; and this evening I would like to discuss whether such a thing is possible at all, and how this absolute steadiness of the mind is to be brought about. I am using the word *absolute* in its correct sense, meaning complete, total control of the mind. As I said, it is essential to have such steadiness because in that state there is no conflict, no dissipation, no distraction of any kind; therefore, it brings enormous energy, and such a mind, being completely steady, is capable of deep, radical penetration into reality.

Now, however much it may control, dominate, discipline itself, can a petty mind ever be steady? Most of our minds are narrow, limited, prejudiced, petty, and a petty mind is occupied incessantly with things that are very superficial—with a job, with quarrels, with resentment, with the cultivation of virtues, with trying to understand something, with gossip, with its own evolution and its own problems. And can such a mind, however much it may control, discipline itself, ever be free to be steady? Because without freedom, the mind obviously cannot be steady.

That is, a mind which is striving after success, a result, groping after something which it cannot have, is essentially narrow, conditioned, limited, made petty by that very effort; and however much it may attempt to be steady by controlling itself, can such a mind ever bring about that essential energy which comes with deep, fundamental steadiness, or will it only build another series of limitations, further pettiness? I hope I am making the problem clear.

If my mind is nationalistic, bound by innumerable beliefs, superstitions, fears, caught up in envy, in resentment, in the cruelty of words, of gesture, thought, however much it may try to think of something beyond itself, it is still limited. So the problem is how to break up this pettiness of the mind, is it not? That is one of the fundamental issues, and if it is clear, then we can proceed to find out what it means to have complete control of the mind.

To find out what is truth, what is God, or whatever name you may like to give it, one must obviously have enormous energy, and in search of that energy, we do all kinds of nonsensical things. Either we resort to monasteries or become cranky about food, or we try to control the various passions, lusts, hoping thereby to canalize energy in order to find something beyond the mind. After all, that is what most of us are endeavoring to do in different ways. We are trying to control our thoughts, our desires, cultivate virtue, be watchful of our words, our actions, and so on, either with the intention of being good, respectable citizens or in the hope of canalizing all this extraordinary vitality of desire in order to find out what lies beyond; but we cannot find that out, however much we may struggle, as long as we do not understand the pettiness of the mind. When a petty mind seeks God, its God will also be petty, obviously; its virtues will be mere respectability. So, is it possible to break up this pettiness? Is the question clear? All right, then let us proceed.

Our minds are petty, envious, acquisitive, fearful, whether we admit it or not. Now, what makes the mind petty? Surely, the mind is narrow, limited, shallow, petty, as long as it is acquisitive. It may give up worldly things and become acquisitive in the pursuit of knowledge, wisdom, but it is still petty because in acquiring, it develops the will to achieve, to gain, and this very will to achieve constitutes pettiness.

May I say something here about attention? Attention is very important, but attention is entirely different from concentration or absorption in something. A child is absorbed in a toy; the toy attracts him, and so he gives his mind to the toy. That is what happens, is it not? The object draws the mind, absorbs the mind, or else the mind absorbs the object. If you are interested in something, the object of that interest is so enticing that it absorbs you; whereas, if you deliberately concentrate on something, which is another form of absorption, then you absorb the object, do you not?

Now, I am talking of something entirely different. I am talking of an attention in which there is no object at all, no strain, no conflict, an attention in which you are neither absorbed nor are you trying to concentrate on something. In listening to what is being said here, you are endeavoring to understand, your listening has an object; therefore, there is an effort, a strain; there is no relaxed attention at all. That is a fact, is it not? If you want to listen to something, there must be no strain, no effort, no object which attracts your attention and absorbs you; otherwise, you are merely hypnotized by what is being said, by a personality, and all the rest of that nonsense. If you observe closely this process of absorption, you will see that in it, there is always a conflict, a sense of strain, an effort to get something; whereas, in attention there is no particular object at all—you are just listening as you would listen to distant music or to the notes of a song. In that state you are relaxed, attentive; there is no strain.

So, if I may suggest, try just being attentive while you are listening to what is being said here. What I am talking about may be difficult and somewhat new and therefore rather disturbing, but if you can listen with this relaxed attention, you won't be mentally agitated though you may be disturbed in a different way, which perhaps is good. What I am saying is something which is essential to understand. I am saying that the mind must be completely steady. But this steadiness cannot come about if the mind tries to make itself steady because the mind, the maker of effort, is in its very nature petty. The mind may be full of encyclopedic knowledge, it may be capable of clever discussions and possess vast accumulations of technique, but it remains essentially petty as long as it is based on the sense of acquisitiveness and therefore on the cultivation of will—that is, as long as there is the 'I', the entity who is acquiring, who is making an effort, who is putting aside and gathering. The mind may think of God, it may discipline itself, try to control its various desires in order to be virtuous, in order to have more energy to seek truth, and so on; but such a mind is narrow, limited—it can never be free and therefore steady.

Our problem, then, is how to break up this pettiness of the mind. Is the question clear? If it is clear, then what are you to do? One sees the necessity of a very steady, deep, quiet mind, a mind which is completely controlled—but not controlled by a separate entity who says, "I must control it." Do you follow? That is, I see the importance of a steady mind. Now, how is this steadiness to be brought about? If another part of the mind says, "I must have a steady mind," then it develops conflicts, controls, subjugations, does it not? One part of the mind dictates to the other part, trying to prevent it from wandering, controlling it, shaping it, disciplining it, suppressing various forms of desire; so there is conflict all the time, is there not?

Now, a mind in conflict is in its very essence petty because its desire is to acquire something. Desiring to acquire a steady mind, you say, "I must control my mind, I must shape it, I must push away all conflicting desires," but as long as there is this dual process in your thinking, there must be conflict, and that very conflict indicates pettiness because that conflict is the outcome of the desire to gain something. So, can the mind obliterate, forget this whole process of acquisition, of acquiring a very steady mind in order to find God, or whatever it is? That is, as you listen, can you see the truth of what is being said immediately? I am saying that there must be complete and absolute steadiness of the mind, and that any endeavor to achieve that state indicates a mind that is divided, a mind that says, "By Jove, I must have that steadiness, it will be marvelous," and then pursues that state through discipline, through control, through various forms of sanction, and so on. But if the mind is capable of listening to the truth of that statement, if it sees the absolute necessity of complete control, then you will find there is no endeavor to achieve a state.

Is this too difficult? I'm afraid it is because, you see, most of us think in terms of effort; there is always the entity who is making an effort to achieve a result, and hence there is conflict. You hear the statement that the mind must be absolutely steady, controlled, or you have read and thought about it, and you say, "I must have that state," so you pursue it through control, discipline, meditation, and so on. In that process there is effort, there is conformity, the following of a pattern, the establishment of authority, and the various other complications that arise. Now, any effort to achieve a result, any form of desire to acquire a state, makes for a petty mind, and such a mind can never possibly be free to be steady. If one sees the truth of that very clearly, then is there not an absolute steadiness of the mind? Do you understand?

To put it differently, one can see very clearly that energy is needed for any form of action. Even if you want to be a rich man, you must devote your life to it, you must give to it your concentrated energy. And to find that which is beyond the activities, the movements of the mind—which implies a tremendous depth in self-knowledge—concentrated energy is essential. Now, how is this concentrated energy to come into being? Seeing the necessity of it, we say, "I must control my temper, I must eat the right food, I must not be over sexual, I must control my passions, my lusts, my desires"—you know, we go off at tangents. These are all tangents because the center is still petty. As long as the mind thinks in terms of acquiring something, of achieving a result, it is ambitious, and an ambitious mind is in its very nature small, shallow. Such a mind, like that of an ambitious man in this world, obviously has a certain amount of energy, but what we are discussing demands much deeper, wider, more unlimited energy in which the self is totally absent.

So, one has been conditioned through centuries—religiously, socially, and morally—to control, to shape one's mind to a particular pattern, or to follow certain ideals, in order to conserve one's energy; and can such a mind break free from all that without effort and come immediately to that state in which the mind is totally still, completely steady? Then there is no such thing as distraction. Distraction exists only when you want to go in a certain direction. When you say, "I must think about this and nothing else," then everything else is a distraction. But when you are completely attentive with that attention in which there is no object because there is no process of acquiring, no cultivation of the will to achieve a result, then you will find that the mind is extraordinarily steady, inwardly still—and it is only the still mind that is free to discover or let that reality come into being.

J. Krishnamurti

Questioner: How can one stop habits?

Krishnamurti: If we can understand the whole process of habit, then perhaps we shall be able to stop the formation of habits. Merely to stop a particular habit is comparatively easy, but the problem is not then solved. All of us have various habits of which we are either conscious or unconscious, so we have to find out whether the mind is caught in habit, and why the mind creates habits at all.

Is not most of our thinking habitual? From childhood we have been taught to think along a certain line, whether as a Christian, a communist, or a Hindu, and we dare not deviate from that line because the very deviation is fear. So fundamentally our thinking is habitual, conditioned; our minds function along established grooves, and naturally there are also superficial habits which we try to control.

Now, if the mind ceases altogether to think in habits, then we shall approach the problem of a superficial habit entirely differently. Do you understand? If you are investigating, trying to find out whether your mind thinks in habits, if that is what you are really concerned with, then the habit of smoking, for example, will have quite a different meaning. That is, if you are interested in inquiring into the whole process of habit, which is at a deeper level, you will treat the habit of smoking in a totally different manner. Being inwardly very clear that you really want to stop, not only the habit of smoking, but the whole process of thinking in habits, you do not fight the automatic movement of picking up a cigarette, and all the rest of it, because you see that the more you fight that particular habit, the more life you give to it. But if you are attentive, completely aware of the habit without fighting it, then you will see that that habit ceases in its time; therefore, the mind is not occupied with that habit. I do not know if you are following this.

Inwardly I see very clearly that I want to stop smoking, but the habit has been set going for a number of years. Shall I fight that habit? Surely, by fighting a habit, I am giving life to it. Please understand this. Anything I fight, I am giving life to. If I fight an idea, I am giving life to that idea; if I fight you, I am giving you life to fight me. I must see that very clearly, and I can see it very clearly only if I am looking at the whole problem of habit, not just at one specific habit. Then my approach to habit is at a different level altogether.

So the question now is: Why does the mind think in terms of habit, the habit of relationship, the habit of ideas, the habit of beliefs, and so on? Why? Because essentially it is seeking to be secure, to be safe, to be permanent, is it not? The mind hates to be uncertain, so it must have habits as a means of security. A mind that is secure can never be free from habit, but only the mind that is completely insecure—which doesn't mean ending up in an asylum or a mental hospital. The mind that is completely insecure, that is uncertain, inquiring, perpetually finding out, that is dying to every experience, to everything it has acquired, and is therefore in a state of not-knowing—only such a mind can be free of habit, and that is the highest form of thinking.

Questioner: Is it possible to raise children without conditioning them, and if so, how? If not, is there such a thing as good and bad conditioning? Please answer this question unconditionally. [Laughter]

Krishnamurti: "Is it possible to raise children without conditioning them?" Is it? I don't think so. Please listen, let's go into this together. But first of all, let's dispose of this latter question, whether there is good conditioning and bad conditioning. Surely, there is only conditioning, not good and bad. You may call it a good conditioning to believe that there is God, but in communist Russia they will say, "What nonsense, that is an evil conditioning." What you call good conditioning, somebody else may call bad, which is obvious, so we can dispose of that question very quickly.

The question is, then, can children be brought up without conditioning, without influencing them? Surely, everything about them is influencing them. Climate, food, words, gestures, conversation, the unconscious responses, other children, society, schools, churches, books, magazines, cinemas—all that is influencing the child. And can you stop that influence? It is not possible, is it? You may not want to influence, to condition your child, but unconsciously you are influencing him, are you not? You have your beliefs, your dogmas, your fears, your moralities, your intentions, your ideas of what is good and what is bad, so consciously or unconsciously you are shaping the child. And if you don't, the school does with its history books that say what marvelous heroes you have and the other fellows haven't, and so on. Everything is influencing the child, so let us first recognize that, which is an obvious fact.

Now, the problem is: Can you help the child to grow up to question all these influences intelligently? Do you understand? Knowing that the child is being influenced all around, at home as well as at school, can you help him to question every influence and not be caught in any particular influence? If it is really your intention to help your child to investigate all influences, then that is extremely arduous, is it not? Because it means questioning, not only your authority, but the whole problem of authority, of nationalism, of belief, of war, of the army—you know, investigating the whole thing, which is to cultivate intelligence. And when there is that intelligence so that the mind no longer merely accepts authority or conforms through fear, then every influence is examined and put aside; therefore, such a mind is not conditioned. Surely, that can be done, can it not? And is it not the function of education to cultivate that intelligence which is capable of examining objectively every influence, of investigating the background, the immediate as well as the deep background, so that the mind is not caught in any conditioning?

After all, you are conditioned by your background; you are this background, which is made up of your Christian inheritance, of the extraordinary vitality, energy, progress of America, of innumerable influences—climatic, social, religious, dietetic, and so on. And can you not look at all that intelligently, bring it out, put it on the table and examine it, without going through the absurd process of keeping what you think is good and throwing out what you think is bad? Surely, one has to look objectively at all of this so-called culture. Cultures create religions but not the religious man. The religious man comes into being only when the mind rejects culture, which is the background, and is therefore free to find out what is true. But that demands an extraordinary alertness of mind, does it not? Such a person is not an American, an Englishman, or a Hindu but a human being; he does not belong to any particular group, race, or culture and is therefore free to find out what is true, what is God. No culture helps man to find out what is true. Cultures only create organizations which bind man. Therefore, it is important to investigate all this, not only the conscious conditioning, but much more the unconscious conditioning of the mind. And the unconscious conditioning cannot be examined superficially by the conscious mind. It is only when the conscious mind is completely quiet that the unconscious conditioning comes out, not at any given moment, but all the time—when you are on a walk, riding in a bus, or talking to somebody. When the intention is to find out, then you will see that the unconscious conditioning comes pouring out, so the doors are open to discovery.

Questioner: When I first heard you speak and had an interview with you, I was deeply disturbed. Then I began watching my thoughts, not condemning or comparing, and so on, and I somewhat gathered the sense of silence. Many weeks later, I again had an interview with you and again received a shock, for you made it clear to me that my mind was not awake at all, and I realized that I had become somewhat smug in my achievement. Why does the mind settle down after each shock, and how is this process to be broken up?

Krishnamurti: Socially, religiously, and personally, we are constantly avoiding any form of change, are we not? We want things to go on as they are because the mind hates to be disturbed. When it achieves something, there it settles down. But life is a process of challenge and response, and if there is no response adequate to the challenge, there is conflict. In order to avoid that conflict, we settle down in comfortable grooves and so decay. That is a psychological fact.

That is, life is a challenge; everything in life is demanding a response, but because you have your limitations, your worries, your conditioning, your beliefs, your ideals of what you should and should not do, you cannot respond to it fully; therefore, there is conflict. In order to avoid or to overcome that conflict, you settle back, you do something else which gives you comfort. The mind is seeking continuously a state in which there will be no disturbance at all, which you call peace, God, or what you like; but essentially the desire is not to be disturbed. The state of nondisturbance you call peace, but it is really death. Whereas, if you understand that the mind must be in a state of continuous response, and there is therefore no desire for comfort, for security, no mooring, no anchorage, no refuge in belief, in ideas, in property, and all the rest of it, then you will see that you need no shock at all. Then there is not this process of being awakened by a shock only to fall asleep again.

You see, that brings up a question which is really very important. We think we need teachers, gurus, leaders, who will help us to keep awake. Probably that is why most of you are here—you want another to help you to keep awake. When somebody can help you to keep awake, you rely on that person, and then he becomes your teacher, your guide, your leader. He may be awake—I do not know—but if you depend on him, you are asleep. [*Laughter*] Please don't laugh it away because this is what we all do in our life. If it is not a leader, it's a group or a family or a book or a gramophone record.

So, is it possible to keep awake without any dependence at all, either on a drug, on a guru, on a discipline, on a picture, or on anything else? In experimenting with this, you may make a mistake, but you say, "That doesn't matter, I am going to keep awake." But this is a very difficult thing to do because you depend so much on others. You have to be stimulated by a friend, by a book, by music, by a ritual, by going to a meeting regularly, and that stimulation may keep you temporarily awake, but you might just as well take a drink. The more you depend on stimulation, the duller the mind gets, and the dull mind must then be led, it must follow, it must have an authority or it is lost.

So, seeing this extraordinary psychological phenomenon, is it not possible to be free from all inward dependence on any form of stimulation to keep us awake? In other words, is not the mind capable of never being caught in a habit? Which means, really, goodbye to whatever we have understood, whatever we have learned, goodbye to everything that we have gathered of yesterday so that the mind is again fresh, new. The mind is not new if it hasn't died to all the things of yesterday, to all the experiences, to all the envies, resentments, loves, passions, so that it is again fresh, eager, awake, and therefore capable of attention. Surely, it is only when the mind is free from all sense of inward dependence that it can find that which is immeasurable.

"If one is capable of studying, watching oneself, one begins to discover how cumulative memory is acting on everything one sees; one is forever evaluating, discarding or accepting, condemning or justifying, so one's experience is always within the field of the known, of the conditioned. But without cumulative memory as a directive, most of us feel lost, we feel frightened, and so we are incapable of observing ourselves as we are. When there is the accumulative process, which is the cultivation of memory, our observation of ourselves becomes very superficial. Memory is helpful in directing, improving oneself, but in self-improvement there can never be a revolution, a radical transformation. It is only when the sense of self-improvement completely ceases, but not by volition, that there is a possibility of something transcendental, something totally new coming into being."

It is an obvious fact that human beings demand something to worship. You and I and many others desire to have something sacred in our lives, and either we go to temples, to mosques, or to churches, or we have other symbols, images, and ideas which we worship. The necessity to worship something seems very urgent because we want to be taken out of ourselves into something greater, wider, more profound, more permanent, so we begin to invent Masters, teachers, divine beings in heaven or on the earth; we devise various symbols—the cross, the crescent, and so on. Or, if none of that is satisfactory, we speculate about what lies beyond the mind, holding that it is something sacred, something to be worshiped. That is what happens in our everyday existence, as I think most of us are well aware. There is always this effort within the field of the known, within the field of the mind, of memory, and we never seem able to break away and find something sacred that is not manufactured by the mind.

So this morning I would like, if I may, to go into this question of whether there is something really sacred, something immeasurable, which cannot be fathomed by the mind. To do that, there must obviously be a revolution in our thinking, in our values. I do not mean an economic or social revolution, which is merely immature; it may superficially affect our lives, but fundamentally it is not a revolution at all. I am talking of the revolution which is brought about through self-knowledge—not through the superficial self-knowledge which is achieved by an examination of thought on the surface of the mind, but through the profound depths of self-knowledge.

Surely, one of our greatest difficulties is this fact that all our effort is within the field of recognition. We seem to function only within the limits of that which we are capable of recognizing—that is, within the field of memory—and is it possible for the mind to go beyond that field? Memory is obviously essential at a certain level. I must know the road from here back to where I live. If you ask me a question about something with which I am very familiar, my response is immediate.

Please, if I may suggest, observe your own mind as I am talking because I want to go into this rather deeply, and if you merely follow the verbal explanation without applying it immediately, the explanation will have no significance whatsoever. If you listen and say, "I will think about it tomorrow or after the meeting," then it is gone, it has no value at all; but if you give complete attention to what is being said and are capable of applying it, which means being aware of your own intellectual and emotional processes, then you will see that what I am saying has significance immediately.

As I was saying, there is an instantaneous response to anything that you know intimately; when a familiar question is asked, you reply easily, the reaction is immediate. And if you are asked a question with which you are not very familiar, then what happens? You begin to search in the cupboards of memory; you try to recall what you have read or thought about it, what your experience has been. That is, you turn back and look at certain memories which you have acquired because what you call knowledge is essentially memory. But if you are asked a question of which you know nothing at all so that you have no referent in memory, and if you are capable of replying honestly that you do not know, then that state of not-knowing is the first step of real inquiry into the unknown.

That is, technologically we are extraordinarily well-developed; we have become very clever in mechanical things. We go to school and learn various techniques, the "know-how" of putting engines together, of mending roads, of building airplanes, and so on, which is but the cultivation of memory. With that same mentality, we wish to find something beyond the mind, so we practice a discipline, follow a system, or belong to some stupid religious organization; and all organizations of that kind are essentially stupid, however satisfactory and gratifying they may temporarily be.

Now, if we can go into this matter together—and I think we can if we give our attention to it—I would like to inquire with you whether the mind is capable of putting aside all memory of technique, all search into the known for that which is hidden. Because, when we seek, that is what we are doing, is it not? We are seeking in the field of the known for that which is not known to us. When we seek happiness, peace, God, love, or what you will, it is always within the field of the known because memory has already given us a hint, an intimation of something, and we have faith in that. So our search is always within the field of the known. And even in science, it is only when the mind completely ceases to look into the known that a new thing comes into being. But the cessation of this search into the known is not a determination; it does not come about by any action of will. To say, "I shall not look into the known but be open to the unknown," is utterly childish, it has no meaning. Then the mind invents, speculates; it experiences something which is absolute nonsense. The freedom of the mind from the known can come about only through self-knowledge, through the revolution that comes into being when every day you understand the meaning of the self. You cannot understand the meaning of the self if there is the accumulation of memory which is helping you to understand the self. Do you understand that?

You see, we think we understand things by accumulating knowledge, by comparing. Surely, we do not understand in that way. If you compare one thing with another, you are merely lost in comparison. You can understand something only when you give it your complete attention, and any form of comparison or evaluation is a distraction.

Self-knowledge, then, is not cumulative, and I think it is very important to understand that. If self-knowledge is cumulative, it is merely mechanical. It is like the knowledge of a doctor who has learned a technique and everlastingly specializes in a certain part of the body. A surgeon may be an excellent mechanic in his surgery because he has learned the technique, he has the knowledge and the gift for it, and there is the cumulative experience which helps him. But we are not talking of such cumulative experience. On the contrary, any form of cumulative knowledge destroys further discovery, but when one discovers, then perhaps one can use the cumulative technique.

Surely what I am saying is quite simple. If one is capable of studying, watching oneself, one begins to discover how cumulative memory is acting on everything one sees; one is forever evaluating, discarding or accepting, condemning or justifying, so one's experience is always within the field of the known, of the conditioned. But without cumulative memory as a directive, most of us feel lost, we feel frightened, and so we are incapable of observing ourselves as we are. When there is the accumulative process, which is the cultivation of memory, our observation of ourselves becomes very superficial. Memory is helpful in directing, improving oneself, but in self-improvement there can never be a revolution, a radical transformation. It is only when the sense of self-improvement completely ceases, but not by volition, that there is a possibility of something transcendental, something totally new coming into being.

So it seems to me that as long as we do not understand the process of thinking, mere intellection, mentation, will have little value. What is thinking? Please, as I am talking, watch yourselves. What is thinking? Thinking is the response of memory, is it not? I ask you where you live, and your response is immediate because that is something with which you are very familiar; you instantly recognize the house, the name of the street, and all the rest of it. That is one form of thinking. If I ask you a question which is a little more complicated, your mind hesitates; in that hesitation it is searching in the vast collection of memories, in the record of the past, to find the right answer. That is another form of thinking, is it not? If I ask you a still more complicated question, your mind becomes bewildered, disturbed; and as it dislikes disturbance, it tries in various ways to find an answer, which is yet another form of thinking. I hope you are following all this. And if I ask you about something vast, profound, like whether you know what truth is, what God is, what love is, then your mind searches the evidence of others who you think have experienced these things, and you begin to quote, repeat. Finally, if someone points out the futility of repeating what others say, of depending on the evidence of others, which may be nonsense, then you must surely say, "I do not know."

Now, if one can really come to that state of saying, "I do not know," it indicates an extraordinary sense of humility; there is no arrogance of knowledge; there is no self-assertive answer to make an impression. When you can actually say, "I do not know," which very few are capable of saying, then in that state all fear ceases because all sense of recognition, the search into memory, has come to an end; there is no longer inquiry into the field of the known. Then comes the extraordinary thing. If you have so far followed what I am talking about, not just verbally, but if you are actually experiencing it, you will find that when you can say, "I do not know," all con-ditioning has stopped. And what then is the state of the mind? Do you understand what I am talking about? Am I making myself clear? I think it is important for you to give a little attention to this, if you care to.

You see, we are seeking something permanent—per-manent in the sense of time, something enduring, ever-lasting. We see that everything about us is transient, in flux, being born, withering, and dying, and our search is always to establish something that will endure within the field of the known. But that which is truly sacred is beyond the measure of time; it is not to be found within the field of the known. The known operates only through thought, which is the response of memory to challenge. If I see that, and I want to find out how to end thinking, what am I to do? Surely, I must through self-knowledge be aware of the whole process of my thinking. I must see that every thought, however subtle, however lofty, or however ignoble, stupid, has its roots in the known, in memory. If I see that very clearly, then the mind, when confronted with an immense problem, is capable of saying, "I do not know," because it has no answer. Then all the answers of the Buddha, of the Christ, of the Masters, the teachers, the gurus, have no meaning because if they have a meaning, that meaning is born of the collection of memories, which is my conditioning.

So, if I see the truth of all that and actually put aside all the answers, which I can do only when there is this immense humility of not-knowing, then what is the state of the mind? What is the state of the mind which says, "I do not know whether there is God, whether there is love," that is, when there is no response of memory? Please don't immediately answer the question to yourselves because if you do, your answer will be merely the recognition of what you think it should or should not be. If you say, "It is a state of negation," you are comparing it with something that you already know; therefore, that state in which you say, "I do not know" is nonexistent.

I am trying to inquire into this problem aloud so that you also can follow it through the observation of your own mind. That state in which the mind says, "I do not know," is not negation. The mind has completely stopped searching; it has ceased making any movement, for it sees that any movement out of the known towards the thing it calls the unknown is only a projection of the known. So the mind that is capable of saying, "I do not know," is in the only state in which anything can be discovered. But the man who says, "I know," the man who has studied infinitely the varieties of human experience and whose mind is burdened with information, with encyclopedic knowledge, can he ever experience something which is not to be accumulated? He will find it extremely hard. When the mind totally puts aside all the knowledge that it has acquired, when for it there are no Buddhas, no Christs, no Masters, no teachers, no religions, no quotations; when the mind is completely alone, uncontaminated, which means that the movement of the known has come to an end—it is only then that there is a possibility of a tremendous revolution, a fundamental change. Such a change is obviously necessary, and it is only the few—you and I, or X, who have brought about in themselves this revolution—that are capable of creating a new world, not the idealists, not the intellectuals, not the people who have immense knowledge or who are doing good works; they are not the people. They are all reformers. The religious man is he who does not belong to any religion, to any nation, to any race, who is inwardly completely alone, in a state of not-knowing, and for him the blessing of the sacred comes into being.

Questioner: The function of the mind is to think. I have spent a great many years thinking about the things we all know—business, science, philosophy, psychology, the arts, and so on—and now I think a great deal about God. From studying the evidence of many mystics and other religious writers, I am convinced that God exists, and I am able to contribute my own thoughts on the subject. What is wrong with this? Does not thinking about God help to bring about the realization of God?

Krishnamurti: Can you think about God? And can you be convinced about the existence of God because you have read all the evidence? The atheist has also his evidence; he has probably studied as much as you, and he says there is no God. You believe that there is God, and he believes that there is not; both of you have beliefs, both of you spend your time thinking about God. But before you think about something which you do not know, you must find out what thinking is, must you not? How can you think about something which you do not know? You may have read the Bible, the Bhagavad-Gita, or other books in which various erudite scholars have skillfully described what God is, asserting this and contradicting that; but as long as you do not know the process of your own thinking, what you think about God may be stupid and petty, and generally it is. You may collect a lot of evidence for the existence of God and write very clever articles about it, but surely the first question is: How do you know what you think is true? And can thinking ever bring about the experience of that which is unknowable? Which doesn't mean that you must emotionally, sentimentally, accept some rubbish about God.

So, is it not important to find out whether your mind is conditioned rather than to seek that which is unconditioned? Surely, if your mind is conditioned, which it is, however much it may inquire into the reality of God, it can only gather knowledge or information according to its conditioning. So your thinking about God is an utter waste of time; it is a speculation that has no value. It is like my sitting in this grove and wishing to be on the top of that mountain. If I really want to find out what is on the top of the mountain and beyond, I must go to it. It is no good my sitting here speculating, building temples, churches, and getting excited about them. What I have to do is to stand up, walk, struggle, push, get there, and find out; but as most of us are unwilling to do that, we are satisfied to sit here and speculate about something which we do not know. And I say such speculation is a hindrance, it is a deterioration of the mind, it has no value at all; it only brings more confusion, more sorrow to man.

So, God is something that cannot be talked about, that cannot be described, that cannot be put into words because it must ever remain the unknown. The moment the recognizing process takes place, you are back in the field of memory. Do you understand? Say, for instance, you have a momentary experience of something extraordinary. At that precise moment there is no thinker who says, "I must remember it"; there is only the state of experiencing. But when that moment goes by, the process of recognition comes into being. Please follow this. The mind says, "I have had a marvelous experience, and I wish I could have more of it," so the struggle of the 'more' begins. The acquisitive instinct, the possessive pursuit of the 'more,' comes into being for various reasons—because it gives you pleasure, prestige, knowledge, you become an authority, and all the rest of that nonsense.

The mind pursues that which it has experienced, but that which it has experienced is already over, dead, gone, and to discover that *which is*, the mind must die to that which it has experienced. This is not something that can be cultivated day after day, that can be gathered, accumulated, held, and then talked and written about. All that we can do is to see that the mind is conditioned and through self-knowledge to understand the process of our own thinking. I must know myself, not as I would ideologically like to be, but as I actually am, however ugly or beautiful, however jealous, envious, acquisitive. But it is very difficult just to see what one is without wishing to change it, and that very desire to change it is another form of conditioning; and so we go on, moving from conditioning to conditioning, never experiencing something beyond that which is limited.

Questioner: I have listened to you for many years, and I have become quite good at watching my own thoughts and being aware of everything I do, but I have never touched the deep waters or experienced the transformation of which you speak. Why?

Krishnamurti: I think it is fairly clear why none of us do experience something beyond the mere watching. There may be rare moments of an emotional state in which we see, as it were, the clarity of the sky between clouds, but I do not mean anything of that kind. All such experiences are temporary and have very little significance. The questioner wants to know why, after these many years of watching, he hasn't found the deep waters. Why should he find them? Do you understand? You think that by watching your own thoughts, you are going to get a reward—if you do this, you will get that. You are really not watching at all because your mind is concerned with gaining a reward. You think that by watching, by being aware, you will be more loving, you will suffer less, be less irritable, get something beyond; so your watching is a process of buying. With this coin you are buying that, which means that your watching is a process of choice; therefore, it isn't watching, it isn't attention. To watch is to observe without choice, to see yourself as you actually are without any movement of the desire to change, which is an extremely arduous thing to do; but that doesn't mean that you are going to remain in your present state. You do not know what will happen if you see yourself as you are without wishing to bring about a change in that which you see. Do you understand?

I am going to take an example and work it out, and you will see. Let us say I am violent, as most people are. Our whole culture is violent, but I won't enter into the anatomy of violence now because that is not the problem we are considering. I am violent, and I realize that I am violent. What happens? My immediate response is that I must do something about it, is it not? I say I must become nonviolent. That is what every religious teacher has told us for centuries—that if one is violent one must become nonviolent. So I practice; I do all the ideological things. But now I see how absurd that is because the entity who observes violence and wishes to change it into nonviolence is still violent. So I am concerned, not with the expression of that entity, but with the entity himself. You are following all this, I hope.

Now, what is that entity who says, "I must not be violent"? Is that entity different from the violence he has observed? Are they two different states? Do you understand, sirs, or is this too abstract? It is near the end of the talk, and probably you are a bit tired. Surely, the violence and the entity who says, "I must change violence into nonviolence," are both the same. To recognize that fact is to put an end to all conflict, is it not? There is no longer the conflict of trying to change because I see that the very movement of the mind not to be violent is itself the outcome of violence.

So, the questioner wants to know why it is that he cannot go beyond all these superficial wrangles of the mind. For the simple reason that, consciously or unconsciously, the mind is always seeking something, and that very search brings violence, competition, the sense of utter dissatisfaction. It is only when the mind is completely still that there is a possibility of touching the deep waters.

Questioner: When we die, are we reborn on this earth, or do we pass on into some other world?

Krishnamurti: This question interests all of us, the young and the old, does it not? So I am going into it rather deeply, and I hope you will be good enough to follow, not just the words, but the actual experience of what I am going to discuss with you.

We all know that death exists, especially the older people, and also the young who observe it. The young say, "Wait until it comes, and we'll deal with it"; and as the old are already near death, they have recourse to various forms of consolation.

Please follow and apply this to yourselves; don't put it off on somebody else. Because you know you are going to die, you have theories about it, don't you? You believe in God, you believe in resurrection, or in karma and reincarnation; you say that you will be reborn here, or in another world. Or you rationalize death, saying that death is inevitable, it happens to everybody; the tree withers away, nourishing the soil, and a new tree comes up. Or else you are too occupied with your daily worries, anxieties, jealousies, envies, with your competition and your wealth, to think about death at all. But it is in your mind; consciously or unconsciously, it is there.

First of all, can you be free of the beliefs, the rationalities, or the indifference that you have cultivated towards death? Can you be free of all that now? Because what is important is to enter the house of death while living, while fully conscious, active, in health, and not wait for the coming of death, which may carry you off instantaneously through an accident, or through a disease that slowly makes you unconscious. When death comes, it must be an extraordinary moment which is as vital as living.

Now, can I, can you, enter the house of death while living? That is the problem—not whether there is reincarnation, or whether there is another world where you will be reborn, which is all so immature, so infantile. A man who lives never asks, "What is living?" and he has no theories about living. It is only the half-alive who talk about the purpose of life.

So, can you and I while living, conscious, active, with all our capacities, whatever they be, know what death is? And is death then different from living? To most of us, living is a continuation of that which we think is permanent. Our name, our family, our property, the things in which we have a vested interest economically and spiritually, the virtues that we have cultivated, the things that we have acquired emotionally—all of that we want to continue. And the moment which we call death is a moment of the unknown; therefore, we are frightened, so we try to find a consolation, some kind of comfort; we want to know if there is life after death, and a dozen other things. Those are all irrelevant problems; they are problems for the lazy, for those who do not want to find out what death is while living. So, can you and I find out?

What is death? Surely, it is the complete cessation of everything that you have known. If it is not the cessation of everything you have known, it is not death. If you know death already, then you have nothing to be frightened of. But do you know death? That is, can you while living put an end to this everlasting struggle to find in the impermanent something that will continue? Can you know the unknowable, that state which we call death, while living? Can you put aside all the descriptions of what happens after death which you have read in books, or which your unconscious desire for comfort dictates, and taste or experience that state, which must be extraordinary, now? If that state can be experienced now, then living and dying are the same.

So, can I, who have vast education, knowledge, who have had innumerable experiences, struggles, loves, hates—can that 'I' come to an end? The 'I' is the recorded memory of all that, and can that 'I' come to an end? Without being brought to an end by an accident, by a disease, can you and I while sitting here know that end? Then you will find that you will no longer ask foolish questions about death and continuity—whether there is a world hereafter. Then you will know the answer for yourself because that which is unknowable will have come into being. Then you will put aside the whole rigmarole of reincarnation, and the many fears—the fear of living and the fear of dying, the fear of growing old and inflicting on others the trouble of looking after you, the fear of loneliness and dependency—will all have come to an end. These are not vain words. It is only when the mind ceases to think in terms of its own continuity that the unknowable comes into being.

"If we can discover from what the sense of domination springs, that discovery may answer the question of why we are violent."

Seventh Talk in the Oak Grove
August 27, 1955

One of our greatest problems, it seems to me, is this question of violence and the desire on our part to find peace. I do not think peace can be found without comprehending the whole anatomy of violence. And peace is not something which is the opposite of violence; it is a totally different state; therefore, it cannot be conceived by a mind that is caught up in violence. As most of our lives are entrenched in violence, and most of our thought is hedged about by violence, it seems to me that it is very important to understand this problem, which is very complex and needs a great deal of penetration, insight; and this afternoon I would like, if I can, to go into it.

Strangely, no organized religions, except perhaps Buddhism and Hinduism, have ever stopped wars and put an end to this astonishing antagonism between man and man. On the contrary, some so-called religions have instigated wars and have been responsible for an enormous slaughter of human beings. Our lives, as we examine them daily, are fraught with violence, and why is it that we are violent? From where does violence spring, and can we really put an end to it? It seems to me that one can come to the end of violence—drastically, radically put a stop to it—only when one understands from what source this violence springs. And I would beg of you not merely to listen to my description of violence but rather, in the very process of my talking, to observe the ways of your own thinking and, through the description, perhaps experience directly the issue that lies behind this word *violence*.

Why is it that we are violent, not only as a race, but also as individuals? I do not know if you have ever asked yourself that question. And what is our approach to violence when we look at it, when we are aware of it, when we think about it? Obviously, most of us say it cannot be helped; we are brought up in this particular society which conditions, encourages us to be violent, and so we slur over the problem very briefly and quickly. But let us see if we cannot go below all that and investigate this problem to find out why each one of us has this extraordinary feeling of violence, and whether it is possible to put an end to it, not superficially, but fundamentally, deeply.

Obviously, this culture, this civilization, is based on violence, not only in the Western world, but also in the East; society encourages violence; our whole economic, social, and religious structure is based on it. I am using that word *violence*, not in the superficial sense of anger or animosity only, but to include this whole problem of acquisition, of competition, the desire on the part of the individual as well as the collective to seek power. Surely, that desire breeds violence, does it not? There must be violence as long as I am competing with another, as long as I am ambitious, acquisitive—acquisitive, not only in the worldly sense of being greedy for many things, but acquisitive in a deeper sense of that word, which is to be driven by the urge to become something, to dominate, to have security, an unassailable position.

So, as long as one is seeking power in any form, surely there must be violence. Please do not say, "In a culture that is based on violence, what shall I as an individual do?" I think that question will be answered if you can listen to what is being said and not ask what is to be done. The doing is not important. The action comes, I think, when we understand this whole complex problem of violence. To be eager to act with regard to violence without understanding the desire to be something, the desire to assert, to dominate, to become, is really quite immature. Whereas, if we can understand the whole process of violence and perceive the truth of it, then I think that very perception will bring about an action which is not premeditated and therefore true. I do not know if you are following this.

We see in the world what is happening. Every politician talks about peace, and everything he does is preparing for division, for antagonism, for war. And it seems to me very important that those of us who are really serious about such matters should understand the truth of the problem and not ask what to do—because if we understand the truth of the problem, that very perception of what is true will precipitate an action which is not yours or mine, and of which we cannot possibly envisage or foresee all the implications.

It is an obvious fact that everything we do in this world—socially, economically, and religiously—is based on violence, that is, on the desire for power, position, prestige, in which is involved ambition, achievement, success. The enormous buildings that we put up, the colossal churches, all indicate that sense of power. I wonder if you have noticed these extraordinary buildings and what your reaction is when you see them? They may have beauty, but to me beauty is something entirely different. For beauty there must be austerity and a total abandonment, and there cannot be abandonment if there is any sense of ambition expressing itself as an achievement. When there is austerity, there is simplicity, and only the mind that is simple can abandon itself, and out of this abandonment comes love. Such a state is beauty. But of that we are totally unaware. Our civilization, our culture, is based on arrogance, on the sense of achievement, and in society we are at each other's throats, violently competing to achieve, to acquire, to dominate, to become somebody. These are obvious psychological facts.

Now, why does this state of violence exist? And recognizing this state, can we go beyond it? If we can, then I think we shall be able to penetrate into something entirely different. Let us take, as an example, the desire to dominate. Why do we want to dominate? First of all, are we at all aware, in our relationships and in our attitude towards life, of this sense of domination, this sense of wanting power, position? If we are aware of it, from what does it spring? Do you understand what I am asking? If we can discover from what the sense of domination springs, that discovery may answer the question of why we are violent. We are all violent in the sense that we all in different ways want to be somebody; we are competitive, ambitious, acquisitive; we want to dominate. Those are the outward symptoms of an inward state, and we are trying to find out what that inward state is which makes us do these things. And are we aware of that state at all, or are we merely adjusting to a moral pattern, being ideologically nonviolent, unambitious, without really tackling the source, the root, which makes us do all these things? If we can go into that, then perhaps our approach to the problem of violence will be entirely different. So please listen to what is being said, not with an attitude of, "Oh, is that all?" but rather let it be a self-discovery. If through my talking about it you can discover, actually experience, the thing for yourself, then it will have an extraordinary effect.

Why am I violent? I want to find out. I see that I am violent because socially, religiously, there is this extraordinary urge to be something. That is a fact. In the business world I want to be richer, to be more capable, to be on top, and in the so-called spiritual world I follow an authority who will help me to be something there. So I see that my activities, my thoughts, my relationships are all based on domination, on dependence. When I depend, I must follow an authority, which breeds violence.

Now, I want to understand the whole process of violence and not merely adjust to a social pattern, which is very superficial and not at all interesting. I want to find out if the mind can be totally free from violence, if this whole process can be radically uprooted from the mind. I am really interested in this; I want to find out. I see that mere adjustment of the superficial urges, demands, and influences to a different pattern does not solve the problem. To substitute one social structure for another, to set up a communist society in place of a capitalist society, will not bring about freedom from domination, freedom from violence. I see that, so I am inquiring into myself to find out what is the source of all these extraordinary urges, demands, pursuits, which breed animosity, violence.

Why am I violent, competitive, ambitious, acquisitive? Why is there in me this constant struggle to be, to become? Obviously, I am running away, taking flight from something through ambition, through acquisitiveness, through wanting to be a success. I am afraid of something, which is making me do all these things. Fear is a state of escape. So I am inquiring into what it is that I am really afraid of. I am not for the moment concerned with the fear of darkness, of public opinion, of what somebody may or may not say of me, because all that is very superficial; I am trying to find out what it is that is fundamentally making me afraid, which in turn drives me to be ambitious, competitive, acquisitive, envious, thereby creating animosity and all the rest of it.

Please think with me. First of all, it seems to me that we are very lonely people. I am very lonely, inwardly empty, and I don't like that state; I am afraid of it, so I shun it, I run away from it. The very running away creates fear, and to avoid that fear, I indulge in various kinds of action. There is obviously this emptiness in me, in you, from which the mind is escaping through action, through ambition, through the urge to be somebody, to acquire more knowledge—you know, the whole business of violence. And without running away, can the mind look at this emptiness, this extraordinary sense of loneliness, which is the ultimate expression of the self?—the self being the entity, the self-consciousness which is empty when it doesn't run. Do you understand what I am explaining? If it is not clear, I shall talk about it in a different manner.

After all, the self, the ego, the 'I' is expressing itself through ambition, through acquisitiveness, through envy, through being violent and trying to be nonviolent, and so on. These are all expressions of the 'me'. I see all that, and going behind it, I also see that that very activity of the self arises from this extraordinary sense of emptiness. I do not know if you have noticed that when you have traced the 'I' in all its movements, you come to this point where the mind is totally aware of the self as being completely empty; but the mind has never really looked at this emptiness—it has always run away, taken flight.

Now, if I can understand what this emptiness is, then perhaps I shall be able to solve the problem of violence, but to understand what emptiness is, I must look at it, and I cannot look at it as long as I am running away. It is the very running away which causes fear and precipitates the action of envy, competitiveness, ruthlessness, enmity, and all the rest of it. So, can the mind look at the thing from which it has always run away into action? I hope I am making myself clear.

Aren't you aware that you are lonely, empty? We are not considering what you should do about it. The "what you should do about it" has produced this stupid, chaotic world. I am asking what is back of the desire to do something—which is extremely difficult to discover because the mind has always avoided that central issue. But if the mind can be totally aware of itself as being empty, lonely, which means a complete discovery of the ways of the self which have brought it to that state, then you will find that any action, any action without that understanding must precipitate violence in different forms. Being a mere pacifist or an ideologist who is pro-this and anti-that does not solve the problem. The man who practices nonviolence hasn't solved the problem of violence at all; he is merely practicing an idea, and he has never tackled this deep, fundamental issue from which all action springs.

Now, please watch yourself; do not just follow my description. Can your mind be aware of this emptiness without running away from it? It is because you are empty, lonely, that you want a companion, you want somebody on whom to depend, and that dependence breeds authority, which you follow; so the very following of authority is an indication of violence. Can the mind, seeing the truth of all that, stop running away and look at this emptiness? Do you understand what it means to look? You cannot look at this emptiness if you are frightened of it, if you want to avoid it; you can be fully aware of it only when there is no sense of condemnation. Please follow this closely. I am going into it slowly, deliberately, so that our communication and understanding can be equal.

I am aware that I am lonely, empty, and I am watching that emptiness, but I cannot watch it if I condemn it. The very condemnation is a distraction from watching. Now, can I watch, be aware of it, without giving it a name? Do you understand? And when I do not give it a name, is the observer who watches it different from that which he watches? It is only when the watcher gives it a name that there is a division, isn't it? Do you follow? Goodness! I'll make it simpler.

When I say, "I am angry," the very naming of that sensation, that reaction, brings about a duality, does it not? But if I do not name it, then that very thing is myself. Do you understand? Look, I name a feeling because the mind is trained to recognize, to give a label; but if the mind doesn't give a label, then the separation, the division between the observer and the observed disappears. In other words, when naming ceases there is only a state, and in that state there is no separate entity to do something about it. The mind is no longer operating upon that which it wishes to understand; therefore, there is a cessation of the activity of the mind, which in its very nature is violent.

Please, this is not intellectual. Don't say it is too high-flown, too abstract, it is absurd, and all that. I am inquiring, step by step, into the anatomy of violence. Our social structure is based on violence; not only is there violence between nations, but individually we are at each other's throats; we are competitive, ruthless. Now, if I want to understand that whole problem, I must understand the activities of the mind in relation to this thing which I call emptiness, and the moment there is that understanding, I no longer want to be anything. Do you follow? It is the desire to be something that breeds enmity and violence. The idealist who wants to create a perfect utopia is in his very nature violent. The man who is practicing nonviolence is a violent human being because he hasn't really understood the problem; he is dealing with it superficially.

So, I see that as long as the mind is operating in terms of ambition or nonambition, it must create chaos, struggle, misery for itself and for others. And if the mind, going more deeply into the problem, understands the whole process of this urge to be something, then it must inevitably come to the point where it sees that it is seeking an escape from not being anything, which is a state of emptiness. And can I understand that emptiness? Can the mind go into it, taste of it, feel it out? Surely, the mind cannot experience and understand that extraordinary thing that we call emptiness, loneliness, as long as it is in any way condemning it, as long as it wants to reject, dominate, or go beyond it. The mind will reject, dominate that state as long as it is giving it a name; and recognizing, naming, is the very process of the mind.

After all, you cannot think without symbols, without ideas, without words. And can the mind cease to verbalize? Can it let that process come to an end and look at what it has called emptiness without giving it a name or creating an imaginative symbol? And when it does, then is the state which it has called emptiness different from itself? Surely it is not. Then there is only a state in which there is no verbalization, no naming, and therefore the whole activity of the mind which separates, which competes, which breeds antagonism, has come to an end. In that state there is quite a different movement taking place. It is no longer violent. There is a gentleness that cannot be understood by the mind which says, "I must be gentle." All volition has totally ceased, for will is also the outcome of violence.

Questioner: What you say seems so foreign and Oriental. Is such a teaching as yours applicable to our Western civilization which is based on efficiency and progress, and which is raising the standard of living throughout the world?

Krishnamurti: Do you think thought is Oriental and Occidental? Manners may vary. I may eat with my hands in India, another with chopsticks in China, and here you eat in still a different way; but what makes the Oriental outlook different from the Western outlook? Is there a difference? If I were born in America and said the same things that I am saying now, would you say it is Oriental? Perhaps you would say it is mystical, impractical, or eccentric. But the problems are the same, whether in India, in Japan, or here. We are human beings, not Asiatics and Americans, Russians and Germans, communists and capitalists. We all have the same human problems.

Now, what I am saying is applicable, surely, both here and in India. Violence is as much your problem as it is a problem in India. The problem of relationship, of love, of beauty, the problem of bringing about a state of mind in which there will be peace, of creating a society which will not be destructive of itself as well as of others—all that is obviously the concern of each one of us, whether we live in the East or in the West. Here you have the problem of the building up of an army, which is an indication of the deterioration of any society because the very basis of the army is authority, nationalism, security; and it is exactly the same problem in India, in Japan, in Asia. So this arbitrary division of thought as Oriental and Occidental does not exist for one who is really inquiring. The man who is conditioned by an Asiatic outlook or philosophy, and who tells you how to live according to that conditioning, is obviously dividing thought as Oriental and Occidental. But we are talking of something entirely different, which is to free the mind from all conditioning, not shape it according to an Oriental philosophy, which is too childish.

What we are trying to do is to investigate together the extraordinary complexity of our lives and to find out if we can really look at these complex problems very simply, but one cannot look at these problems very simply unless one understands oneself. The self is an extraordinarily complex being with innumerable contradictory desires. We are everlastingly at war within ourselves, and this inner conflict precipitates itself into outer activities. To understand the self—the conscious as well as the unconscious—is an enormous task, and one can only understand it from day to day, from moment to moment. It is a book that never ends; therefore, it is not something to be concluded.

So, if one can listen to what is being said, not as an American, a European, or an Oriental, but as a human being who is directly concerned with all these problems, then together we shall create a different world; then we shall be really religious people. Religion is the search for truth, and for the religious person there is no nationality, no country, no philosophy; he does not follow anybody; therefore, he is really a revolutionary in the most profound sense of the word.

Questioner: Is the release we experience in various forms of self-expression an illusion, or is this sense of fulfillment related to the creativeness of which you speak?

Krishnamurti: Is there such a thing as self-fulfillment at all? We have accepted that there is, have we not? If I am an artist, I must fulfill; if you are a writer, you must fulfill. We are all trying to fulfill ourselves in different ways, through family, through children, through husband or wife, through property, through ideas. If you are ambitious, you must fulfill your ambition; otherwise, you are thwarted, and in that very thwarting there is misery. We are all trying to fulfill ourselves, but we have never asked if there is such a thing as self-fulfillment at all. Surely, the man who is seeking fulfillment is hounded by frustration. That is simple enough, is it not? If I am all the time trying to fulfill through my son, through my wife, through an idea, through action, there is always the shadow of frustration and fear behind it. So if I want to understand fear, frustration, the agony of psychosomatic complexities, and all the rest of it, I must question this whole idea that there is such a thing as fulfilling myself, which is the 'me' trying to become something. May not the 'me' be an illusion, though a reality in the sense that it is operative in action? To the man who is ambitious, competitive, acquisitive, envious, the 'me' is not illusory; it is a very real thing. But to a man who begins to inquire into this whole problem, who really wants to understand what is peace—not the peace of terror, the peace of politicians, nor the peace of self-satisfaction after gathering something which one has longed for, but the peace in which there is no contention, no struggle to be anything—to such a man there comes the experience of being totally nothing, and in that state there is a creativity which is timeless. What we call creativeness is a process of learning a technique and expressing it, but I am talking of something entirely different, of a mind in which the self is totally absent.

Questioner: Does the creativeness of which you speak confine itself to the ecstasy of personal atonement, or might it also liberate one's power to make use of one's own and other men's scientific achievements for the helping of man?

Krishnamurti: Such questions—if this happens, then what will follow?—are obviously put by people who are listening very superficially. As I said, the action of a man who is seeking, and for whom reality comes into being, will be different from that of the man who has had a glimpse of this state and tries to express it. After all, most of us are educated in some kind of technique: painting, engineering, medicine, and so on. That is obviously necessary, but merely learning the mechanics of a particular profession is not going to release this creative thing. Creative reality—call it God, truth, or what you like—comes into being, not through a technique, but only when the mind has understood itself. And do you know how difficult it is to understand oneself? It is difficult because we are dilettantes; we are not really interested. But if you are really aware, if you give your whole attention to understanding yourself, then you will find an indestructible treasure. You don't have to read a single book about philosophy, psychology, analysis, and all the rest of it because you are the total content of all humanity, and without understanding yourself, you will go on creating innumerable problems, endless miseries. To understand oneself requires, not impetuous urges, conclusions, but great patience. One must go slowly, millimeter by millimeter, never missing a step—which doesn't mean that you must everlastingly keep awake. You can't. It does imply that you must watch and drop what you have watched, let it go and pick it up again, so that the mind does not become a mere accumulation of what it has learned but is capable of watching each thing anew. When the mind is capable of looking at itself and understanding itself, then there is that creativeness of reality, and such a mind can use technique without causing misery.

Seventh Talk

Questioner: What is the significance of dreams, and how can one interpret them for oneself?

Krishnamurti: I would like to go into this question rather deeply and not just deal with it superficially, and I hope you are sufficiently interested to follow it step by step.

Most of us dream. There are nightmares from over-eating or from eating the wrong things, but I am not talking of such dreams. I am talking of dreams that have a psychological significance. There are various states in dreaming, are there not? You dream, wake up, and then you try to find the meaning of what you have dreamed—you interpret it. The interpretation depends on your knowledge, on your conditioning, on what you have learned from various philosophers, psychologists, and so on. And if you misinterpret, your whole conclusion will be wrong. Then one may dream, and as one is dreaming, the interpretation is going on at the same time so that one wakes up with clarity; one has understood the dream, and it is no longer influencing one. I do not know if that has happened to you.

So the problem is not how to interpret dreams but why we dream at all. Do you understand? If you interpret your dreams according to any psychologist, then the interpretation depends on his particular conditioning, and if you try to interpret them for yourself, your interpretation is shaped by your own conditioning. In either case the interpretation may be wrong, and any conclusion or action based upon it may therefore prove to be entirely false. So the problem is not how to interpret dreams but why do you dream at all? If you could solve that problem, then interpretation would not be necessary. If you could really understand the whole process of dreaming, then it would become a very simple issue.

Why do we dream? Please, let us think it out together, not according to some authority who has written a book about it. Leave all those things completely aside if you can, and let us think it out together very simply. Why do we dream? What do we mean by dreaming? You go to bed, fall asleep, and while you are asleep, action is going on, taking the form of various symbols or scenes; and on waking you say, "Yes, that is the dream I have had."

Now, what has happened? Please follow this, it is very simple. When you are awake during the day, the superficial mind is occupied with many things—with your job, with quarrels, with children, with money, with going to the market, with washing dishes—you know, it is occupied with dozens of things. But the superficial mind is not the whole mind; there is also the unconscious, is there not? You don't have to read a book to find out that there is an unconscious. Our hidden motives, our instinctual responses, our racial urges, our inherited contradictions, beliefs—they are all there in the unconscious. The unconscious obviously wants to tell the superficial mind something, and as the superficial mind is quiet when it is asleep, the unconscious tries to tell it. The unconscious is also in movement all the time, only it has no opportunity to express anything during the day, so it projects various symbols when the conscious mind is asleep, and then we say, "I have had a dream." It is not complex if you can go into it.

Now, I do not want to occupy myself everlastingly with the interpretation of dreams, which is like being occupied with the kitchen, with God, with drink, with women, or what you will. I want to find out why I dream and whether it is possible not to dream at all. The psychologists may say it is impossible not to dream, but leave the experts to their expertness, and let us find out. [Laughter] No, no, please don't laugh it off. Why are there dreams? And is it possible for dreams to come to an end without suppressing, or trying to go beyond dreaming, so that in sleep the mind is totally still? I want to find out, so that is my first inquiry.

Why do I dream? I dream because my conscious mind is occupied during the day with so many things. But can the conscious mind be open during the day to all the unconscious intimations and promptings? Do you understand? Can the superficial mind be so alert during the day that it is aware of the unconscious motives, the glimpses of the things that are hidden, without trying to suppress them, change them, do something about them? If you can be merely aware, not critically, but choicelessly, of this whole conflict; if you can be open so that the unconscious gives its hints from moment to moment during the day, while you are on the bus or riding in a car, while you are sitting at the table or talking to friends; if you can just watch how you look at somebody, the manner of your speech, the way you treat people who are not of your own quality—then you will find, as you observe deeper, more profoundly, that there is the cessation of dreaming altogether. Then there is no need for intimations, hints, from the unconscious during sleep to tell you what you should or should not do because the whole thing is being revealed as you are living from day to day.

So, we have come to a very interesting point, which is this: During the daytime, the mind is extraordinarily alert, watching without judging, without condemning; and when the whole process of consciousness has been uncovered, examined, and understood, then you will find that in sleep there is a total quietness, and that, being totally quiet, the mind can go to depths which it is not possible for the waking consciousness to touch at any time. Do you understand? I am afraid not. I shall explain again, and I hope you don't mind being a little late.

You see, our search is for happiness, for peace, for God, for truth, and so on; there is a constant struggle to adjust, to love, to be kind, to be generous, to put away this and acquire that. If we are at all aware, we know that to be a fact; there is this total activity of turmoil, of struggle, of adjustment, going on all the time, and a mind in that state can obviously never find anything new. But if I am aware during the day of the various thoughts and motives that arise, if I am aware that I am ambitious, condemning, judging, criticizing, and see the whole of that activity, then what happens? My mind is no longer struggling, it is no longer pushing, there is not that turmoil created by the urge to find. So the mind is completely quiet, not only the superficial mind, but the whole content of consciousness; and in that state of complete quietness in which there is no movement to find, no effort to be or not to be, the mind can touch depths which it can never possibly touch when it is trying to find something. That is why it is very important to be aware without condemnation, to look without criticism, without judgment. And you can do this all day long, off and on, so that the mind is no longer an instrument of struggle when it sleeps, is no longer catching intimations from the unconscious through symbols and trying to interpret them, is no longer inventing the astral plane and all that nonsense. Being free from all conditioning, the mind in sleep is then capable of penetrating into depths which the waking consciousness can never reach, and when you awake, you will find there is a newness totally unexperienced before. It is like shedding the past and being born anew.

"Being free of society implies not being ambitious, not being covetous, not being competitive; it implies being nothing in relation to that society which is striving to be something. But you see, it is very difficult to accept that because you may be trodden on, you may be pushed aside; you will have nothing. In that nothingness there is sanity, not in the other... As long as one wants to be part of this society, one must breed insanity, wars, destruction, and misery; but to free oneself from this society—the society of violence, of wealth, of position, of success—requires patience, inquiry, discovery, not the reading of books, the chasing after teachers, psychologists, and all the rest of it."

I t is quite difficult, I think, to differentiate between the collective and the individual, and to discover where the collective ends and the individual begins, also, to see the significance of the collective, and to find out whether it is at all possible ever to be free from the collective so as to bring about the totality of the individual. I do not know if you have thought about this problem at all, but it seems to me that it is one of the fundamental issues confronting the world, especially at the present time when so much emphasis is being laid on the collective. Not only in the communistic countries, but also in the capitalistic world where welfare states are being created, as in England, more and more significance is being given to the collective; there are collective farms and cooperatives in various forms, and looking at all this, one wonders where the individual comes into the picture and whether there is an individual at all.

Are you an individual? You have a particular name, a private bank account, a separate house, certain facial and psychological differentiations, but are you an individual? I think it is very important to go into this because it is only when there is the incorruptibility of the individual, which I shall discuss presently, that there is a possibility of something totally new taking place. That implies finding out for oneself where the collective ends, if it ends at all, and where the individual begins, which involves the whole problem of time. This is quite a complex subject, and being complex, one must attack it simply, directly, not in a roundabout way; and if I may, I would like to go into it this morning.

Please, if I may suggest, observe your own thinking as I am talking, and do not merely listen with approval or disapproval to what is being said. If you are merely listening with approval or disapproval, with a superficial, intellectual outlook, then this talk and the talks that have taken place will be utterly useless. Whereas, if one is capable of observing the functioning of one's own mind as I am describing it, then that very observation does bring about an astonishing action which is not imposed or compelled.

I think it is very important for each one of us to find out where the collective ends and where the individual begins. Or, though modified by temperament, personal idiosyncrasies, and so on, is the whole of our thinking, our being, the collective? The collective is the conglomeration of various conditionings brought about by social action and reaction, by the influences of education, by religious beliefs, dogmas, tenets, and all the rest of it. This whole heterogeneous process is the collective, and if you examine, look at yourself, you will see that everything you think, your beliefs or nonbelief, your ideals or opposition to ideals, your efforts, your envies, your urges, your sense of social responsibility—all that is the result of the collective. If you are a pacifist, your pacifism is the result of a particular conditioning.

So, if we look at ourselves, it is astonishing to see how completely we are the collective. After all, in the

Western world, where Christianity has existed for so many centuries, you are brought up in that particular conditioning. You are educated either as a Catholic or a Protestant, with all the divisions of Protestantism. And once you are educated as a Christian, as a Hindu, or whatever it be, believing in all kinds of stuff—hell, damnation, purgatory, the only Savior, original sin, and innumerable other beliefs—by that you are conditioned, and though you may deviate, the residue of that conditioning is there in the unconscious. You are forever afraid of hell, or of not believing in a particular savior, and so on.

So, as one looks at this extraordinary phenomenon, it seems rather absurd to call oneself an individual. You may have individual tastes, your name and your face may be quite different from those of another, but the very process of your thinking is entirely the result of the collective. The racial instincts, the traditions, the moral values, the extraordinary worship of success, the desire for power, position, wealth, which breeds violence—surely, all that is the result of the collective, inherited through centuries. And from all this conglomeration is it possible to extricate the individual? Or is it utterly impossible? If we are at all serious in the matter of bringing about a radical change, a revolution, isn't it very important to consider this point fundamentally? Because it is only for the man who is an individual in the sense in which I am using that word, who is not contaminated by the collective, who is entirely alone, not lonely, but completely alone inwardly—it is only for such an individual that reality comes into being.

To put it differently, we start our lives with assumptions, with postulates: that there is or there is not God, that there is heaven, hell, that there must be a certain form of relationship, morality, that a particular ideology must prevail, and so on. With these assumptions, which are the product of the collective, we build a structure which we call education, which we call religion, and we create a society in which rugged individualism is either rampant or controlled. This society is based on the assumption that it is inevitable and necessary to have competition, that there must be ambition, envy. And is it possible not to build on any assumption but to build as we inquire, as we discover? If the discovery is that of somebody else, then we immediately enter the field of the collective, which is the field of authority; but if each one of us starts with freedom from assumptions, from all postulates, then you and I will build a totally different society, and it seems to me that this is one of the most fundamental issues at the present time.

Now, seeing this whole process, not only at the conscious level, but at the unconscious level as well—the unconscious being also the residue of the collective—is it possible to extricate from it the individual? Which means, is it possible to think at all if thinking is stripped of the collective? Is not all your thinking collective? If you are educated as a Catholic, a Methodist, a Baptist, or what you will, your thinking is the result of the collective, conscious or unconscious; your thinking is the result of memory, and memory is the collective. This is rather complex, and one must go into it rather slowly, neither agreeing nor disagreeing; we are trying to find out.

When we say there is freedom of thought, it seems to me such utter nonsense because, as you and I think, thinking is the reaction of memory, and memory is the outcome of the collective—the collective being Christian, Hindu, and all the rest of it. So, there can never be freedom of thought as long as thinking is based on memory. Please, this is not mere logic. Don't brush it aside that way, saying, "Oh well, this is just intellectual logic." It isn't. It happens to be logical, but I am describing a fact. As long as thought is the reaction of memory, which is the residue of the collective, the mind must function in the field of time—time being the continuation of memory as yesterday, today, and tomorrow. For such a mind there is always death, corruptibility, and fear, and however much it may seek something incorruptible, beyond time, it can never find it because its thought is the result of time, of memory, of the collective.

So, can a mind whose thought is the result of the collective, whose thought is the collective, extricate itself from all that? Which means, can the mind know the timeless, the incorruptible, that which is alone, which is not influenced by any society? Don't assert or deny; don't say, "I have had an experience of it"—all that has no meaning because this is really an extraordinarily complex question. We can see that there will always be corruption as long as the mind is functioning in the collective. It may invent a better code of morality, bring about more social reforms, but all that is within the collective influence and therefore corruptible. Surely, to find out if there is a state which is not corruptible, which is timeless, which is immortal, the mind must be totally free from the collective; and if there is total freedom from the collective, will the individual be anticollective? Or will he not be anticollective but will function at a totally different level which the collective may reject? Are you following all this?

J. Krishnamurti

The problem is: Can the mind ever go beyond the collective? If there is no possibility of going beyond the collective, then we must be content with decorating the collective, opening up windows in the prison, installing better lights, more bathrooms, and so on. That is what the world is concerned with, which it calls progress, a higher standard of living. I am not against a higher standard of living; that would be silly, especially if one comes from India where one sees starvation as it is never seen in any other part of the world except perhaps in China, where people have half a meal a day and not even that, where there is sorrow, suffering, disease, and the incapacity to revolt because they are starved. So, no intelligent man can be against a higher standard of living, but if that is all, then life is merely materialistic. Then suffering is inevitable; then ambition, competition, antagonism, ruthless efficiency, war, and the whole structure of the modern world, with occasional witch-hunting and social reform, is perfectly all right. But if one begins to inquire into the problem of sorrow—sorrow as death, sorrow as frustration, sorrow as the darkness of ignorance—then one must question this whole structure, not just parts of it, not just the army or the government, in order to bring about a particular reform. Either one must accept this society in its entirety, or one must reject it completely—reject it, not in the sense of running away from it, but finding out its significance.

So, if there is no possibility for the mind to extricate itself from this prison of the collective, then the mind can only go back and reform the prison. But to me, there is such a possibility because to struggle everlastingly in the prison would be too stupid. And how is the mind to extricate itself from this heterogeneous mass of values and contradictions, pursuits, and urges? Until you do that, there is no individuality. You may call yourself an individual, you may say you have a soul, a higher self, but those are all inventions of the mind which is still part of the collective. One can see what is happening in the world. A new group of the collective is denying that there is a soul, that there is immortality, permanency, that Jesus is the only Savior, and all the rest of it. Seeing this whole conglomeration of assertions and counterassertions, the inevitable question arises: Is it possible for the mind to disentangle itself from it? That is, can there be freedom from time—time as memory, the memory which is the product of any particular culture, civilization, or conditioning? Can the mind be free from all this memory? Not the memory of how to build a bridge, or the structure of the atom, or the way to one's house; that is factual memory, and without it, one would be insane or in a state of amnesia. But can the mind be free from psychological memory? Surely, it can be free only when it is not seeking security. After all, as I was saying yesterday afternoon, as long as the mind is seeking security, whether in a bank account, in a religion, or in various forms of social action and relationship, there must be violence. The man who has much breeds violence, but the man who sees the much and becomes a hermit, he also breeds violence because he is seeking security, not in the world, but in ideas.

The problem is, then: Can the mind be free from memory—not the memory of information, of knowledge, of facts, but the collective memory which has accrued through centuries of belief? If you put that question to yourself with full attention and do not wait for me to answer, because there is no answer, then you will see that as long as your mind is seeking security in any form, you belong to the collective, to the memory of many centuries. And not to seek security is astonishingly difficult because one may reject the collective but develop a collective of one's own experience. Do you understand? I may reject society with all its corruption, with its collective ambition, greed, competitiveness; but having rejected it, I have experiences, and every experience leaves a residue. That residue also becomes the collective because I have collected it; it becomes my security, which I give to my son, to my neighbor, so I again create the collective in a different pattern.

Is it possible for the mind to be totally free from the memory of the collective? That means being free from envy, from competitiveness, from ambition, from dependence, from this everlasting search for the permanent as a means to be secure; and when there is that freedom, only then is there the individual. Then a totally different state of mind and being exists. Then there is no possibility of corruption, of time, and for such a mind, which may be called individual or some other name, reality comes into being. You cannot go after reality; if you do, it becomes your security; therefore, it is utterly false, meaningless, like your pursuing money, ambition, fulfillment. Reality must come to you, and it cannot come to you as long as there is the corruption of the collective. That is why the mind must be completely alone, uninfluenced, uncontaminated, therefore free of time—and only then that which is measureless, timeless, comes into being.

Many questions have been sent in, and unfortunately they cannot all be answered. But what we have done is to select the more representative ones, and I am going to try to answer as many of them as possible this morning.

I hope that you are not being mesmerized by me. Please, what I am saying has meaning; I am not saying it casually. You listen with silence. If that silence is merely the result of being overpowered by another personality, or by ideas, then it is utterly valueless. But if your silence is the natural outcome of your attention in observing your own thoughts, your own mind, then you are not being mesmerized, you are not being hypnotized. Then you do not create a new collective, a new following, a new leader—which is a horror; it has no meaning and is most destructive. If you are really alert, inwardly observant, you will find that these talks will have been worthwhile because they will have revealed the functioning of your own mind. Then you have nothing to learn from another; therefore, there is no teacher, no disciple, no following. The totality of all this is in your own consciousness, and one who describes that consciousness does not constitute a leader. You don't worship a map or the telephone, or the blackboard on which something is written. So this is not the creation of a new group, a new leader, a new following, at least not for me. If you create it, it is your own misery. But if you observe your own mind, which is what the blackboard says, then such observation leads to an extraordinary discovery, and that discovery brings its own action.

Questioner: Many people who have been through the shat-tering experience of war seem unable to find their place in the modern world. Tossed about by the waves of this chaotic society, they drift from one occupation to another and lead a miserable life. I am such a person. What am I to do?

Krishnamurti: If you are in revolt against society, what generally happens? Through compulsion, through necessity, you conform to a particular social pattern, and so you have an everlasting battle within yourself and with society. Society has made you what you are; it has brought about wars, destruction. This culture is based on envy, turmoil; its religions do not make a religious man. On the contrary, they destroy the religious man. Then what is an individual to do? Having been shattered by war, either you become a neurotic, or you go to somebody who will help you to be nonneurotic and fit into the social pattern, thereby continuing a society that breeds insanity, wars, and corruption. Or else—which is really very difficult—you observe this whole structure of society and are free of it. Being free of society implies not being ambitious, not being covetous, not being competitive; it implies being nothing in relation to that society which is striving to be something. But you see, it is very difficult to accept that because you may be trodden on, you may be pushed aside; you will have nothing. In that nothingness there is sanity, not in the other. The moment you see that, the moment you are as nothing, then life looks after you. It does. Something happens. But that requires immense insight into the whole structure of society. As long as one wants to be part of this society, one must breed insanity, wars, destruction, and misery; but to free oneself from this society—the society of violence, of wealth, of position, of success—requires patience, inquiry, discovery, not the reading of books, the chasing after teachers, psychologists, and all the rest of it.

Questioner: I am puzzled by the phrase you used in last week's talk, "a completely controlled mind." Does not a controlled mind involve will or an entity who controls?

Krishnamurti: I did use that expression "a controlled mind," and I thought I had explained what I meant by it. I see it has not been understood, so I shall explain again.

Isn't it necessary to have, not a controlled mind, but a very steady mind, a mind that has no distractions? Please follow this. A mind that has no distractions is a mind for which there is no central interest. If there is a central interest, then there are distractions. But a mind that is completely attentive, not towards a particular object, is a steady mind.

Now, let us examine briefly this whole question of control. When there is control, there is an entity who controls, who dominates, who sublimates or finds a substitute. So in control there is always a dual process going on—the one who controls, and the thing that is controlled. In other words, there is conflict. Surely, you are aware of this. There is the controller, the evaluator, the judge, the experiencer, the thinker, and opposed to him there is the thing which he examines, controls, suppresses, sublimates, and all the rest of it. So there is always a battle going on between these two—the one that is, and the one that says, "I must be." This contradiction, this conflict, is a waste of energy. And is it possible to have only the fact and not the controller? Is it possible to see the fact that I am envious without saying that it is wrong to be envious, that it is antisocial, antispiritual, and must be changed? Can the entity who evaluates totally disappear and only the fact remain? Can the mind look at the fact without evaluation, that is, without opinion? When there is an opinion about a fact, then there is confusion, conflict. I hope you are following all this.

So, confusion is a waste of energy, and the mind must be confused as long as it approaches the fact with a conclusion, with an idea, with an opinion, with a judgment, with condemnation. But when the mind sees the fact as true without opinion, then there is only the perception of the fact, and out of that comes an extraordinary steadiness and subtlety of mind because there is then no deviation, no escape, no judgment, no conflict in which the mind wastes itself. So there is only thinking, not a thinker, but the experiencing of that is very difficult.

Look what happens. You see a lovely sunset. At the precise moment of seeing it, there is no experiencer, is there? There is only the sense of great beauty. Then the mind says, "How beautiful that was. I would like to have more of it," so the conflict begins of the experiencer wanting more. Now, can the mind be in a state of experiencing without the experiencer? The experiencer is memory, the collective. Oh, do you see it? And can I look at the sunset without comparing, without saying, "How beautiful that is. I wish I could have more of it"? The 'more' is the creation of time, in which there is the fear of ending, the fear of death.

Questioner: Is there a duality between the mind and the self? If there is not, how is one to free the mind from the self?

Eighth Talk

Krishnamurti: Is there a duality between the 'me', the self, the ego, and the mind? Surely not. The mind is the self, the ego. The ego, the self, is this urge of envy, of brutality, of violence, this lack of love, this everlasting seeking of prestige, position, power, trying to be something—which is what the mind is also doing, is it not? The mind is thinking all the time how to advance itself, how to have more security, how to have a better position, more comfort, greater wealth, increased power, all of which is the self. So the mind is the self; the self is not a separate thing, though we like to think it is because then the mind can control the self; it can play this game of back and forth, subjugating, trying to do something about the self—which is the immature play of an educated mind, educated in the wrong sense of that word.

So, the mind is the self; it is this whole structure of acquisitiveness, and the problem is: How is the mind to be free of itself? Please follow this. If it makes any movement to free itself, it is still the self, is it not?

Look, I and my mind are the same; there is no division between myself and my mind. The self that is envious, ambitious, is exactly the same as the mind that says, "I must not be envious, I must be noble," only the mind has divided itself. Now, when I see that, what am I to do? If the mind is the product of environment, of envy, greed, conditioning, then what is it to do? Surely, any movement it makes to free itself is still part of that conditioning. All right? Do you understand? Any movement on the part of the mind to free itself from conditioning is an action of the self which wants to be free in order to be more happy, more at peace, nearer the right hand of God. So

I see the whole of this, the ways and trickeries of the mind. Therefore the mind is quiet, it is completely still, there is no movement; and it is in that silence, in that stillness, that there is freedom from the self, from the mind itself. Surely, the self exists only in the movement of the mind to gain something or to avoid something. If there is no movement of gaining or avoiding, the mind is completely quiet. Then only is there a possibility of being free from the totality of consciousness as the collective and as opposed to the collective.

Questioner: Having seriously experimented with your teachings for a number of years, I have become fully aware of the parasitic nature of self-consciousness and see its tentacles touching my every thought, word, and deed. As a result, I have lost all self-confidence as well as all motivation. Work has become drudgery and leisure, drabness. I am in almost constant psychological pain, yet I see even this pain as a device of the self. I have reached an impasse in every department of my life, and I ask you as I have been asking myself: What now?

Krishnamurti: Are you experimenting with my teachings, or are you experimenting with yourself? I hope you see the difference. If you are experimenting with what I am saying, then you must come to, "What now?" because then you are trying to achieve a result which you think I have. You think I have something which you do not have, and that if you experiment with what I am saying, you also will get it—which is what most of us do. We approach these things with a commercial mentality—I will do this in order to get that. I will worship, meditate, sacrifice in order to get something.

Now, you are not practicing my teachings. I have nothing to say. Or rather, all that I am saying is: Observe your own mind, see to what depths the mind can go; therefore, you are important, not the teachings. It is important for you to find out your own ways of thinking and what that thinking implies, as I have been trying to point out this morning. And if you are really observing your own thinking, if you are watching, experimenting, discovering, letting go, dying each day to everything that you have gathered, then you will never put that question, "What now?"

You see, confidence is entirely different from self-confidence. The confidence that comes into being when you are discovering from moment to moment is entirely different from the self-confidence arising from the accumulation of discoveries, which becomes knowledge and gives you importance. Do you see the difference? Therefore, the problem of self-confidence completely disappears. There is only the constant movement of discovery, the constant reading and understanding, not of a book, but of your own mind—the whole, vast structure of consciousness. Then you are not seeking a result at all. It is only when you are seeking a result that you say, "I have done all these things, but I have got nothing, and I have lost confidence. What now?" Whereas, if you are examining, understanding the ways of your own mind without seeking a reward, an end, without the motivation of gain, then there is self-knowledge, and you will see an astonishing thing come out of it.

Questioner: How can one prevent awareness from becoming a new technique, the latest fashion in meditation?

Krishnamurti: As this is a very serious question, I am going into it rather deeply, and I hope you are not too tired to follow with relaxed alertness the workings of your own mind.

It is important to meditate, but what is still more important is to understand what is meditation; otherwise, the mind gets caught in mere technique. Learning a new trick of breathing, sitting in a certain posture, holding your back straight, practicing one of the various systems for silencing the mind—none of that is important. What is important is for you and me to find out what is meditation. In the very finding out of what is meditation, I am meditating. Do you understand? Take it easy, sirs, don't agree or disagree.

It is enormously important to meditate. If you do not know what meditation is, it is like having a flower without scent. You may have a marvelous capacity to talk or to paint or to enjoy life; you may have encyclopedic information and correlate all knowledge, but those things will have no meaning at all if you do not know what meditation is. Meditation is the perfume of life; it has immense beauty. It opens doors that the mind can never open; it goes to depths that the merely cultured mind can never touch. So meditation is very important. But we always put the wrong question and therefore get a wrong answer. We say, "How am I to meditate?" so we go to some swami, some foolish person, or we pick up a book, or follow a system, hoping to learn how to meditate. Now, if we can brush all that aside, the swamis, the yogis, the interpreters, the breathers, the "sitting-stillers," and all the rest of it, then we must inevitably come to this question: What is meditation?

Eighth Talk

So, please listen carefully. We are now asking, not how to meditate, or what the technique of awareness is, but what is meditation?—which is the right question. If you put a wrong question, you will receive a wrong answer, but if you put the right question, then that very question will reveal the right answer. So, what is meditation? Do you know what meditation is? Don't repeat what you have heard another say, even if you know somebody, as I do, who has devoted twenty-five years to meditation. Do you know what meditation is? Obviously you don't, do you? You may have read what various priests, saints, or hermits have said about contemplation and prayer, but I am not talking of that at all. I am talking of meditation—not the dictionary meaning of the word, which you can look up afterwards. What is meditation? You don't know. And that is the basis on which to meditate. [*Laughter*] Please listen, don't laugh it off. "I don't know." Do you understand the beauty of that? It means that my mind is stripped of all technique, of all information about meditation, of everything others have said about it. My mind does not know. We can proceed with finding out what is meditation only when you can honestly say that you do not know; and you cannot say, "I do not know," if there is in your mind the glimmer of secondhand information, of what the Gita or the Bible or Saint Francis has said about contemplation or the results of prayer—which is the latest fashion; in every magazine they are talking about it. You must put all that aside because if you copy, if you follow, you revert to the collective.

So, can the mind be in a state in which it says, "I do not know"? That state is the beginning and the end of meditation because in that state every experience—every experience—is understood and not accumulated. Do you understand? You see, you want to control your thinking, and when you control your thinking, hold it from distraction, your energy has gone into the control and not into thinking. Do you follow? There can be the gathering of energy only when energy is not wasted in control, in subjugation, in fighting distractions, in suppositions, in pursuits, in motivations; and this enormous gathering of energy, of thought, is without motion. Do you understand? When you say, "I do not know," then there is no movement of thought, is there? There is a movement of thought only when you begin to inquire, to find out, and your inquiry is from the known to the known. If you don't follow this, perhaps you will think it out afterwards.

Meditation is a process of purgation of the mind. There can be purgation of the mind only when there is no controller; in controlling, the controller dissipates energy. Dissipation of energy arises from the friction between the controller and the object he wishes to control. Now, when you say, "I do not know," there is no movement of thought in any direction to find an answer; the mind is completely still. And for the mind to be still, there must be extraordinary energy. The mind cannot be still without energy—not the energy that is dissipated through conflict, suppression, domination, or through prayer, seeking, begging, which implies a movement, but the energy that is complete attention. Any movement of thought in any direction is a dissipation of energy, and for the mind to be completely still, there must be the energy of complete attention. Only then is there the coming into being of that which is not to be invited,